The Canadian Legislative System

The Canadian Legislative System

Politicians and Policy-Making

Robert J. Jackson
and
Michael M. Atkinson

Canadian Controversies Series

Macmillan of Canada / 1974

ISBN 0-7705-0959-2 Cloth
0-7705-0960-6 Paper

Library of Congress Catalogue Card No. 73-92684

Printed in Canada

Contents

Canadian Controversies Series

Canadian political commentators have adopted the full range of political styles, from cold detachment to partisan advocacy. The Canadian Controversies Series is disciplined by the idea that while political analysis must be based on sound descriptive and explanatory modes of thought, social scientists should not abnegate the role of evaluating political systems. Such evaluations require a conscious approach to the interrelationships between facts and values, empirical and normative considerations in politics.

Each theme in the series has been chosen to illustrate some basic principles of Canadian political life and to allow the respective authors freedom to develop normative positions on the related problems. It is thus hoped that the volumes will stimulate debate and advance public understanding of some of the major questions which confront the Canadian political system. By treating the enduring themes and problems in Canada, the authors will also illustrate the important contribution that social science can offer to politics in terms of facts, ideas, theories and comparative frameworks within which meaningful controversy can take place. Creative political thought must not be divorced from the political fabric of a country but form an integral part of it.

ROBERT J. JACKSON,
General Editor

Preface

This volume is disciplined by the philosophy of the Canadian Controversies Series that political analysts should not abdicate the role of evaluating political systems. *The Canadian Legislative System: Politicians and Policy-Making* combines descriptive, analytic and evaluative statements about the polity. It places the legislative system within the framework of Canadian culture and dissects the major institutions in the inner circle and Parliament in order to ascertain the role played by politicians in the policy-making process. The volume concludes that major adjustments are required if Canadian parliamentarians are to secure a major position in the system.

There has been a considerable amount of research on the Canadian political system and many of our perspectives have been based on this work. The contributions of Peter Aucoin, Bruce Doern, David Falcone, David Kwavnick, John Meisel, Khayyam Paltiel, Robert Presthus, John Porter, Michael Stein, Michael Whittington and Richard Van Loon on Canadian politics in general were invaluable. Detailed examinations of legislative behaviour by Allan Kornberg, David Hoffman and Norman Ward provided important information for the various sections on political actors. The institutional and procedural research of William Dawson, Thomas Hockin, Ned Franks, J. R. Mallory, Roman March, Michael Rush, Denis Smith, John Stewart and Paul Thomas underlies many of the descriptive statements about Parliament and its committees.

We have been blessed with the editorial assistance of Diane Mew. As executive editor of this series on Canadian politics and society Diane's encouragement and technical competence have played a major part in bringing our book to fruition.

The bulk of the material in the book is designed to express opinions the authors developed during work undertaken for the Canadian government over the past several years. In this respect, we are grateful for opportunities provided to witness parts of the inner circle in operation and to study the detailed functioning of the House of Commons. We are indebted to those senior officials who generously answered specific and general questions about the legislative system. Among those who deserve special thanks are Gerard Bertrand, Michael Butler, Henry Davis, Peter Dobell, Michael Kirby, Philip Laundy, Marcel Massé, André Millar, Robert Miller, C. R. Nixon, Michael Pitfield, Jim Ryan, Eric Spicer, Donald Thorson and Len Trudel.

In terms of the development of our perspective on reform we have been aided by politicians and their appointees. These include members or former members of Parliament — Allan J. MacEachen, John Reid, Mark MacGuigan, Douglas Fisher, Gordon Blair, Gordon Fairweather, Stanley Knowles, Grant Deachman, Jim Jerome, Lloyd Francis and Robert Kaplan. The political assistants include Brian Bruce, Gloria Kunka, Sandy Blue, Jerry Yanover, Robert Wright, Jim Davey and Peter McGuire.

The academics, bureaucrats and politicians are responsible neither for the facts we have cited nor the judgments put forward. Many of them, however, are in positions to weigh the evidence and decide whether or not there is a case for restructuring the role of politicians in the policy-making process. We hope that our book will contribute to such a reassessment.

ROBERT J. JACKSON
MICHAEL M. ATKINSON
Tabarka, Tunisia

The Canadian Legislative System

1. Perspectives on the Canadian Legislative System

It is fashionable nowadays to forecast the kind of institutions and resources that society will have in the year 2000. This is normally accomplished by statistical models which project current trends into the future. If such is attempted for the Canadian legislative system one point seems certain of discovery—it will not become more important! Increased governmental activity, the significance of federal-provincial arrangements, and the ascendancy of the Prime Minister and his office will continue to prevent the growth of parliamentary influence.

The question of weak legislative power is not unique to Canada. In the United Kingdom, the United States and other democracies critics have professed that their political systems have not achieved a proper balance of constitutional and political forces. While in the American case this judgment is normally concluded from an examination of the intentions of the founding fathers, scholars in parliamentary systems of the British type often refer to a "classic" and harmonious period from which Parliament has declined. The legislature constantly emerges as the weak partner in the constitutional balance.

The list of indictments against the Canadian Parliament is impressive, as we will attempt to show. Yet it would be presumptuous to argue that in the Canadian political system Parliament has "declined." The relative authority and power of legislatures is a complex question. To begin an assessment requires, above all, a clear conception of the purposes of Parliament in the political system. Part of our concern in this book is to characterize and assess some of the activities Parliament is expected to perform. Our task is also to set the Canadian Parliament within the larger legislative system. In fact, it is this comprehensive framework which is our main concern, since relations among elements such as cabinet, Parliament and the bureaucracy determine the kinds of functions each can be expected to undertake. The role of politicians can be properly assessed only when Parliament is integrated with the other institutions in the policy-making process.

Unfortunately, there is no comprehensive study of the relations between the Canadian Parliament and the executive that would guide an appraisal of the legislative system. Canadians tend to measure their institutions against the positive features of the British model and against the dangers assumed to be inherent in the American congressional system. There are limitations as well as advantages to this perspective. To some extent the Canadian experience does parallel the British and many of the criticisms of parliamentary government apply to both. But the Canadian legislative system has some peculiar burdens and in our opinion its capacity for flexibility has never been very impressive.

An appreciation of the evolution of the Canadian legislative system can best be obtained by a brief comparison with British constitutional development. The paramount political question in Britain during the eighteenth and first half of the nineteenth centuries was the quest for parliamentary democracy. The gradual absorption of democratic ideals in the culture was mirrored by the growing importance of Parliament in society. In the second half of the nineteenth century democratic reformers concentrated on extending the franchise from property owners to all male citizens and eventually to females. Westminster institutions were exported to the colonies in the belief they would provide the same stable foundation they had in Great Britain.

During the embryonic stages of the British Parliament the government did not dominate in the development of legislation. The private act of Parliament was the normal vehicle for law-making. This was congruent with the type of society and government that existed in Britain. Walkland put it this way: "Procedure by Private Bill was natural to a society which wished to make marginal adjustments to the reigning state of affairs, but which could not conceive of consciously-directed broad social and economic reform."[1] However, the consensus on limited government could not persist indefinitely. New constitutional arrangements were emerging in the latter part of the eighteenth and early nineteenth centuries and these would eventually contribute to the more active intervention of government in society.

The Reform Act of 1832 acknowledged the existence of a new and delicate balance of constitutional forces. J. S. Mill's earlier distinction between the function of governing and that of controlling the governors emerged as the key to understanding the new developments.[2] The responsibility of ministers to Parliament was confirmed and defeat in the House of Commons on important legislative proposals required the government to resign. At the same time, however, parliamentary interference with ministerial responsibilities diminished.

By the 1860s the constitutional balance had been changed again. Political parties had become national organizations which could command the support of the electorate. Most candidates had to rely on the parties for electoral success. At the same time governments began to accept responsibility for a legislative program. In the face of new societal demands the public general act of Parliament became the main legislative instrument and private bills declined to insignificance. In Parliament procedure began to solidify, generally in the direction of increased governmental control. The significance of cabinet continued to grow and the civil service showed a remarkable ability to remain in touch with modern developments.

While governments in Britain were tightening their control over Parliament and parliamentary procedure, the first few decades of the Canadian Confederation more closely approximated earlier periods of British constitutional development.[3] Until about the turn of the century, private and private members' bills predominated in the Canadian House of Commons. Parliamentary leadership relied on the extensive patronage at its disposal to attract and secure the support it needed. Gradually parliamentary parties became identifiable, but until 1878 members of Parliament could not always be relied upon to maintain their party loyalties. During this period John A. Macdonald suffered several defeats at the hands of Parliament without submitting his resignation. At the same time there was little acceptance of the need for wholesale government intervention in the economy, except, of course, for the promotion of railways as a stimulus to economic development.

By the end of the nineteenth century Canadian political parties were becoming national in scope.[4] They were not the mass organized parties that had come to dominate the British political system but they had begun to aggregate demands and to organize the vote in the electoral process. The parties began to limit the independence of MPs and to extinguish any desire for wholesale changes in the relations between the executive and Parliament. Patronage was by no means unknown but it was limited by the growth of a permanent civil service.

With the expansion in the economy there was an immense growth in government expenditure and activity. In 1913 the executive began the slow process of establishing control over the consultative process and decision-making. A procedure to terminate debate—closure—was introduced at this time, and other rules guaranteed that the government's expenditure proposals would be discussed on a more regular basis.

On a general level the institutions of the Canadian legislative system developed in the same direction as those in Britain. Cabinet's responsibility for initiating public policy became undisputed, parties replaced patronage as the means of securing legislative support for the executive, and periodic procedural changes provided governments with more opportunities to realize their legislative programs. However, the Canadian legislative system has never corresponded exactly to the British. Each system has had unique institutional arrangements. There have been obvious differences in the Speakership, for example, and in the operation of parliamentary committees. More important, perhaps, have been the differences in the institutional and cultural context of parliamentary government.

Parliamentary institutions in Canada have not been stabilized and strengthened by a homogeneous political culture as they were in Britain. Religious, linguistic and regional cleavages have deterred politicians from the task of building centralized political institutions. Canadian parliamentary institutions have not become arenas for the disposal of local, provincial and regional claims. Instead, new institutions capable of sustaining intergovernmental liaison have been created to satisfy these demands of the federal system.[5]

Societal cleavages have also fragmented the party system in Canada and affected parliamentary organization. The existence of minor parties has complicated the legislative process and created some impediments to reform. Minority government is perhaps the most significant legacy of minor parties. While little research has been undertaken on the impact of minority government, it is clear that party leaders prefer not to seek procedural changes during periods of parliamentary instability. Furthermore, reform requires some degree of consensus on the role of Parliament in the political system and alternating minority-majority situations militate against such agreement.

When the House of Commons embarked on reform in the 1960s most commentators agreed on the advisability of a review.[6] Institutional reform and attitudes toward procedures had not kept pace with changes in the volume and complexity of the nation's business. One expert has suggested that, prior to these reforms, procedures in the Canadian Parliament were reminiscent of those at Westminster before the reforms of the 1880s.[7]

Reform proved to be a long and sometimes disjointed process. Its history illustrates how far Canadian parliamentary institutions had lagged behind other policy-making structures and how a vast overhaul was bound to elicit grievances and suspicions from some individuals and from others hope for more extensive change. The Special Committees on Procedure throughout the 1960s offered proposals designed to modernize antiquated methods and to make greater use of institutions such as parliamentary committees.[8] After these reforms were finalized in 1969 some academics began to argue that they constituted an unnecessary strengthening of the executive and were evidence of presidential aspirations on the part of the Prime Minister.[9] But as soon as this period of reform was complete, many MPs began to request the extensive support facilities that had long been associated exclusively with the American congressional system.

Disillusionment with existing parliamentary institutions and skepticism about the democratic process is not limited to Canada. In most developed democracies scholars lament executive dominance, administrative despotism and parliamentary decline, and continually stress the insignificant role of the backbencher in policy-making.[10] Everywhere the demands placed on the time of legislators are mounting. The necessity for personal specialization and more legislative expertise engulfs most parliamentarians. At the same time interest groups rather than political parties have become prominent participants in the creation and administration of public policy. The role of the representative is being questioned and specific problems like administrative secrecy and political corruption have acquired new urgency. There has also been a general weakening in acceptance of the rational model of democracy, in which voters are expected to influence policy decisions by their electoral choices. Empirical research on voting behaviour has increased doubts about the democratic potential of legislative institutions.[11] In short, once the battle for representative assemblies had been won many critics found that the new institutions could not satisfy all their democratic expectations.

In response to these alleged deficiencies in liberal democracies some democrats have demanded a reconsideration of the concept of representation. They advocate a decentralization of authoritative decision-making in order that citizens can participate directly in the process of law-making. Such participatory democracy, it is expected, will produce better citizens and improve decisions.[12] Since democracy implies a reasonable degree of citizen participation, the demand for an increase is bound to be well received. However, there are several problems involved in elevating direct citizen participation to the summit of the hierarchy of democratic values. First, advocates of participatory democracy are usually unclear about the meaning of participation or about the degree and type which is most desirable. Second, they have been unable to suggest what mechanisms or structures would actually improve the individual's access to policy-making machinery. Third, they have been unable to demonstrate convincingly that citizens wish to assume the burden of continual involvement in national decision-making. Most citizens seem content to engage in the political process through elections and occasionally through the traditional devices of direct participation such as initiative, referendum and recall.

The orthodox response to criticisms of representative democracy has come from those who support the reform of parliamentary institutions. From the most trenchant critics have come some of the most vigorous proposals for change. Occasionally, romantic allusions are made to more glorious days of Parliament,[13] but reformers have generally concentrated on procedural changes and the enhancement of particular parliamentary institutions. Unfortunately, procedural reforms are often piecemeal and regarded as ends in themselves. When such reforms are contemplated ultimate objectives are seldom paramount and the consequent incrementalism has occasionally led to inconsistent proposals. Furthermore, it is by no means clear which of these reforms will actually have an impact on the effectiveness of representative institutions. And the evaluation of all reforms is impossible in the absence of a coherent philosophy about the functions of the legislative system and the institutions which comprise it.

The detailed criticisms of the legislative system contained in this book and the reform package offered in the last chapter are firmly in the "reform of Parliament" tradition. The conceptualization of the legislative system and the description of particular institutions is designed to integrate criticisms and proposals. To guide our discussion, however, it is useful to outline a set of reform priorities based on a preliminary evaluation of Canada's experience with parliamentary institutions.

First, the balance of power between Parliament and the executive must be reconsidered. In Canada the executive too often assumes a posture of complacency toward the legislature. In part this is attributable to Parliament's inability to hold the executive responsible for the ever-increasing scope of government activities, to control the commitments made at federal-provincial conferences and to compete with the personalized politics of the Prime Minister. In the House of Commons the governing party continually supports executive action while the opposition parties cannot be relied upon to offer a comprehensive alternative. The weakness of parliamentary institutions is accentuated when the bureaucracy, the cabinet and the Prime Minister establish direct links of communication with the public. To some extent task forces, royal commissions and public opinion polls have replaced parliamentarians as feedback mechanisms to the executive.

Second, the member of Parliament ought to become a more important participant in the legislative system. In part this means improving the politician's role in policy-making and strengthening the links between the citizen and his representative. Traditional executive-legislative divisions need to be re-evaluated and the gulf which presently separates representatives and their constituents must be narrowed by an improvement in parliamentary communications.

Third, parliamentarians and academics must reconsider the relations between the legislative system and Canadian society. In particular, attention ought to be paid to the general feelings Canadians have about their parliamentary institutions. Legislatures in industrialized nations do not always command universal support and it is by no means certain that all Canadians have a benevolent view of legislative activities. If the Canadian legislature lacks prestige (and we believe that it does), part of the problem may be traced to an inability to canvass the various alternatives of public policy. It must compete with other political structures which are more proficient in the generation and communication of new political ideas. In order to attract public support, Parliament will have to function as a forum where members assemble, not merely to pass legislation but, as Walter Bagehot declared, to inform, teach and express the nation.

In the next chapter a conceptual framework of the legislative system in a parliamentary setting is outlined and the relationships between the legislature, the executive and society are discussed in general terms. Only when attention is directed toward these complex interrelations is it possible to achieve an adequate perspective. The linkages between the environment and the legislative system are discussed in chapter three. In this case, precision is hampered by the lack of research and the tendency of Canadian scholars to concentrate on the demand side of the relationship. Chapter four focuses on the pre-parliamentary part of the legislative system. Among those structures examined are the cabinet, the Prime Minister's Office, the Privy Council Office and the Department of Justice. Chapters five and six concentrate on the parliamentary part of the system, its operation and some of the obstacles to a more adequate performance of its functions. Research on Canadian legislators is examined in chapter seven, particularly the aspirations of Canadian members of Parliament and their opportunities for personal initiative. The problems of evaluating the Canadian legislative system are considered in chapter eight, and chapter nine discusses our reform proposals and assesses the likelihood of systematic change.

NOTES

1. S. A. Walkland, *The Legislative Process in Great Britain* (London: Allen and Unwin, 1968), pp. 9 and 14.
2. For an authoritative discussion, see M. J. C. Vile, *Constitutionalism and the Separation of Powers* (London: Oxford University Press, 1967), Chapter 8.
3. This theme is developed by Ronald Blair in "What Happens to Parliament?", in T. Lloyd and J. McLeod, eds., *Agenda: 1970* (Toronto: University of Toronto Press, 1968), pp. 217-240.
4. See Escott M. Reid, "The Rise of National Parties in Canada," in Hugh Thorburn, ed., *Party Politics in Canada,* 1st edition (Toronto: Prentice-Hall, 1963), pp. 14-21; and George M. Hougham, "The Background and Development of National Parties," in ibid., pp. 1-13.
5. The incompatability of federal and parliamentary forms of government is discussed in Richard Simeon, *Federal-Provincial Diplomacy* (Toronto: University of Toronto Press, 1971), pp. 25-31. See also Donald Smiley, *Canada in Question: Federalism in the Seventies* (Toronto: McGraw-Hill Ryerson, 1972), Chapter 3.
6. There has not been a general book on this topic in Canada. Discussions of reform can be found in the following: Thomas Hockin, "Reforming Canada's Parliament: The 1965 Reforms

and Beyond," *Canadian Bar Review,* Vol. XVI, no. 2 (1966), pp. 326-345; Donald Page "Streamlining the Procedures of the Canadian House of Commons," *Canadian Journal of Economics and Political Science,* Vol. 33, no. 1, (February 1967), pp. 27-49; C. E. S. Franks, "The Reform of Parliament," *Queens Quarterly,* Vol. 76, no. 1, (Spring 1969), pp. 113-117; Pauline Jewett, "The Reform of Parliament," *Journal of Canadian Studies,* Vol. 1, (1966), pp. 11-16; Philip Laundy, "Procedural Reform in the Canadian House of Commons," in R. S. Lankster and D. Dewol, eds., *The Table: Being the Journal of the Society of Clerks-at-the-Table in Commonwealth Parliaments for 1965,* Vol. 34, (London: Butterworth, 1966); Trevor Lloyd, "The Reform of Parliamentary Proceedings," in Abraham Rotstein, ed., *The Prospect of Change: Proposals for Canada's Future* (Toronto: McGraw-Hill, 1965), pp. 23-39; J. A. A. Lovink, "Who Wants Parliamentary Reform,"? *Queens Quarterly,* Vol. 79, no. 4, (Winter 1972), pp. 502-513; and J. A. A. Lovink, "Parliamentary Reform and Governmental Effectiveness," *Canadian Public Administration,* Vol. 16, no. 1, (Spring 1973), pp. 35-54.

7. Laundy, "Procedural Reform in the Canadian House of Commons," p. 20.
8. Special Committee on Procedure, *Third Report* (Ottawa: Queen's Printer, 1968).
9. Denis Smith, "President and Parliament: The Transformation of Parliamentary Government in Canada," in O. Kruhlak, *et al.,* eds., *The Canadian Political Process,* (Toronto: Holt, Rinehart and Winston, 1970), pp. 367-382.
10. For comparison with the Canadian literature see the following books: On the British Parliament: Michael Foot, *Parliament in Danger* (London: Pall Mall, 1965); Bernard Crick, *The Reform of Parliament* (London: Weidenfeld and Nicolson, 1964); A. H. Hanson and B. Crick, eds., *Commons in Transition* (London: Fontana, 1970); and P. G. Richards, *The Backbenchers* (London: Faber and Faber, 1973). On the American Congress: John Saloma III, *Congress and the New Politics* (Boston: Little, Brown, 1970); Roger Davidson, David Kovenock and Michael O'Leary, *Congress in Crisis: Politics and Congressional Reform* (Belmont, Calif., Wadsworth Publishing Co., 1966); James MacGregor Burns, *Congress on Trial* (New York: Gordian Press, Inc., 1966); and Joseph S. Clark, ed., *Congressional Reform: Problems and Prospects* (New York: Thomas Y. Crowell Co., 1965). On the French Parliament: André Chandernagor, *Un Parlement, Pour Quoi Faire?* (Paris: Gallimard, 1967); J-Ch. Maout and R. Muzellec, *Le Parlement Sous le Ve République*

(Paris: Colin, 1971); Pierre Avril, *Les Français et leur Parlement* (Paris: Casterman, 1972); Jean-Luc Parodi, *Les Rapports Entre le Legislatif et l'Executif Sous La Cinquième République* (Paris: Colin, 1972).

11. Seminal works in the field of voting behaviour include: A. Campbell, P. E. Converse, W. E. Miller, and D. E. Stokes, *The American Voter* (New York: John Wiley & Sons, 1960) and David Butler and Donald Stokes, *Political Change in Britain* (Toronto: Macmillan, 1969). On the relationship between constituents and legislators, see Warren Miller and Donald Stokes, "Constituency Influence in Congress," *American Political Science Review,* Vol. 57, no. 1 (March 1963), pp. 45-56, and Kenneth Prewitt and Heinz Eulau, "Political Matrix and Political Representation: Prolegomenon to a New Departure from an Old Problem," *American Political Science Review,* Vol. 63, no. 2 (June 1969), pp. 427-441.
12. Participatory democracy is normally discussed in the context of democratic theory. One of those who places emphasis on the need for increased participation is Peter Bachrach. See *The Theory of Democratic Elitism: A Critique* (Boston: Little, Brown, 1967). A balanced collection of views can be found in Terrance E. Cook and Patrick M. Morgan, eds., *Participatory Democracy* (New York: Harper and Row, 1971).
13. See, for example, Andrew Hill and Anthony Whichelow, *What's Wrong With Parliament?* (London: Penguin Books Ltd., 1964).

2. The Legislative System and Policy-Making: An Overview

The problems in the legislative system are intimately related to other processes and parts of society. The task of this chapter is to provide an overview of the legislative system which will be sensitive to the fact that legislatures do not operate in isolation from other societal or political processes, and that they may produce results or outputs unnoticed by formal-legal methods of analysis. In Canada we have inherited a legacy of facts that can be used to guide such an overview. In a detailed, but piecemeal, fashion the structures of policy-making have been exposed to view. Civil servants have given us a view of the Treasury Board and the Privy Council Office, and even the Prime Minister's Office has been discussed, albeit from a height at which the facts may not be verified. Academics have examined the role of standing committees in the House of Commons, political leadership in Canada, royal commissions and advisory councils. But perhaps our most valuable knowledge has come from those who have been intimately involved with Parliament. A generation of Canadian scholars has been tutored in the rules of the Canadian House of Commons, the constitution and the role of the Governor General. In short, many Canadian legislative institutions have been given a microscopic treatment. However, in Canada, much of the analysis has been inward-looking and although the evolution of our institutions has been analysed we have failed to examine the legislative system as a whole or to see trends and anticipate problems.

To help place legislative problems in a comparative and manageable perspective we will rely on the concept of system.

Practitioners of systems analysis in political science endorsed this concept after becoming uncomfortable about discussing politics in terms of formal institutions and legal procedures. In Canada, politicians and political scientists are still inclined to view legislative elements in isolation and to treat their problems as legal and inherently different. The concept of system, on the other hand, is illuminating primarily because it presumes the interconnectedness of parts and depicts the elements on that basis. This approach is not the only way of examining politics, but systems analysts have demonstrated that it can facilitate understanding of complex processes and provide a complement to traditional constitutional descriptions. It is in the context of facilitating understanding that we bring this concept to bear, first on politics in general and then on the Canadian legislative system.

THE POLITICAL SYSTEM

In their preliminary examinations of the political system, academics utilize almost exclusively the model developed by David Easton. This approach is based on a biological analogy which seeks to portray the whole as more than the sum of its parts. In the political system the parts are not individuals, but subsystems, roles and structures. The idea of a system suggests relationships between these parts and the whole. In Easton's approach the political system is seen as only one part of the social system and the study of politics is essentially the study of the authoritative allocation of values for society. His approach focuses attention on the input-output exchange which links the political system and its environment. The key elements are depicted in Figure 1, with the exception of stress which is communicated to the system through fluctuations in the level of inputs.

Inputs from the environment may be described very generally as demands or supports. The model suggests that demands are made on the polity but they also originate within the polity itself. The campaigns for better housing and increased social welfare which have been prevalent in postwar Canada are examples of demands on the polity. Demands which arise within the policy-making structures (such as the

Figure 1

THE POLITICAL SYSTEM

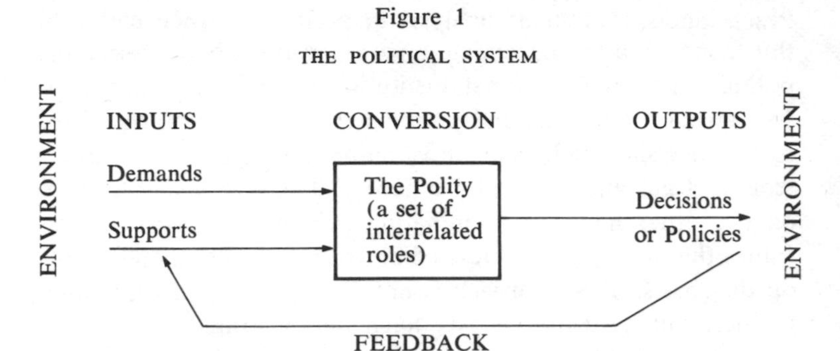

SOURCE: Adapted from David Easton, *A Systems Analysis of Political Life* (New York: John Wiley and Sons, 1965), p. 32.

public service or cabinet) are sometimes referred to as withinputs. The nature of each demand is rooted firmly in the culture and the economic and social structure of the environment. Successful conversion of demands into outputs depends upon such factors as their acceptance in the environment, the importance of the originators of the demands, the timing of the demands and the means by which they are pressed upon the political system.

In theory one could create a demand schedule and estimate the likelihood of success for each demand or group of demands. The demands are regulated by "gatekeepers" in the system. In Canada structures such as parties, interest groups and communications networks operate as gatekeepers by selecting and conditioning which demands will be processed by the political system. Since every demand cannot be satisfied by the resources available, it is important that not all become issues. Such a situation would undoubtedly overtax the system's capacity and result in unmanageable stress.

Basic to the continued activity of the system is the support directed toward the three components of the polity: the community, regime and government. Citizens must be willing to settle differences through peaceful action and this presumes their acceptance of the political community. Support must also be directed toward the regime, that is the rules of the game through which resources are authoritatively allocated. Finally, support may be directed toward the government—that is, the individuals who hold the highest offices in the regime and are responsible for its decisions and policies.

The level of overall support determines the system's capacity to process demands. Supports include actual material resources such as money, time and labour. The taxes paid to government and the time and energy used in participating in political parties are examples of this form of input. Support also consists of those actions or attitudes which affirm allegiance to the political system. The pro-regime attitudes expressed in a public opinion poll in October 1970, when the government employed the War Measures Act, may be taken as a general example of this type of support.

Different political cultures provide different types and degrees of support, but the level of support is also affected by the outputs and the extent to which demands are satisfied by the political system. The attitudes and norms which individuals adopt toward the political system are transmitted on a continuing basis through the socialization process. Coercion will, of course, provide some degree of compliance in the political system, but alone it can never be sufficient. The political stability of the system requires a moral consensus in addition to central coercive mechanisms.

It is easy to recognize that outputs from the political system could have an effect on the level of support the system enjoys. The most important outputs are the policies adopted in reaction to the issues which have entered the system. Policies determine future decisions and structure the nature of future system outputs. The decision to build a railway across Canada required a commitment regarding how resources and support would be mobilized for decades. While some outputs allocate and mobilize tangible resources, others are symbolic. Symbolic outputs would include the adoption of a national flag for Canada and a new national anthem.

THE LEGISLATIVE SYSTEM

Implicit in traditional writing about politics is the assumption that the legislature is the keystone of democracy. In this book, however, the legislative system is seen simply as a major subsystem of the political system. It competes with interest groups, parties, the bureaucracy and provincial governments in the importance it plays in the political system.

The legislative system must be distinguished from the courts, administrative agencies, and other governmental activities. All may force citizens to comply with laws and regulations. Without determining here the specific activities within its sphere, or the exact nature of the outputs involved, the legislative system can be said to include those structures and interrelated roles involved in the initial creation of a legislative program through to those which provide the formal proclamation of laws. The term "process" will be used to refer to the on-going linear means of creating these products of the system. While such definitions aid in the identification of institutions and behaviours which are important in the legislative system, they do not exhaust the activities that take place in the structures. For example, surveillance of the administration and communication with the public are activities of the legislative system which are not specifically part of law-making.

The legislative system should be considered part of what has been called the "policy-making process." Policies are grand and general in scope. In academic discourse they are distinguished from decisions by the requirement that they set the parameters of future decisions by developing a long-term perspectives in issue areas. Of course, decisions may constitute policies, either singly or cumulatively. However, not every decision should be considered a policy. The decision to provide a particular Opportunities for Youth grant or a Local Initiative Project is not a policy, but the decision to establish such programs was a policy decision. Policy-making is the activity of arriving at these types of significant decisions. In the study of the legislative system the language of policy-making has some advantages over the use of the word "law-making." Since all the components of a policy may be present without the formalities attached to passing a bill in Parliament, the word "policy" can be used to apply to almost any government action. Such policies as bilingualism in the public service and multiculturalism required no legislation. Money may be appropriated for programs through votes on the estimates without the passage of a substantive bill. Many policies, such as reorganization within government departments and a vast number of regulations which are made and applied by the bureaucracy, are not even discussed in Parliament.

The study of policy-making has produced several competing models of how the process operates. Students of policy-making use them sometimes to describe the process and sometimes to suggest how the process ought to work. Important among these models are the incremental, the rational, and the mixed-scanning models.[1] Most Canadian students of policy-making seem to agree that at least until 1968 the process at the federal level was best represented by the incremental model, which emphasizes the creation of new policy by modification of past activities. However, there have been recent efforts to consciously create the institutions of rational policy-making in Canada. Prime Minister Trudeau appeared to believe that the needs of Canadian society could best be met by the establishment of new institutions for the efficient pursuit of generalized goals.

The contents of policies differ remarkably and various attempts have been made to categorize these political outputs and to relate them to other variables. Theodore Lowi classifies public policies as distributive, redistributive or regulatory.[2] Distributive policies are those which confer benefits on an individual basis to groups in the political system. The distributed resources are disaggregated and dispensed in small units, like patronage. Only by accumulation are such decisions considered policies. Canadian examples include the choice of post office sites and the building of federal airports and wharves. Redistributive policies are those which require governments to indulge one major group in society and deny another. In Canada such policies are not aimed directly at individuals but at social categories or classes. Examples include policies, such as the progressive tax system, which are designed to alleviate economic inequality. Regulatory policy tends to be the residue of overt group conflict for benefits all cannot share. The conflict which characterizes this type of policy-making is based on shifting coalitions of groups. The anticombines legislation, which was successfully opposed by large manufacturing concerns, affords a good example of Canadian regulatory policy and the conflict it inspires.

Another type of output may be called positional policy. Such policy is intended to have an impact on political actors, the structures, or the dominant values of policy-making. Its importance for the political system cannot be exaggerated. In Canada efforts to restructure federal-provincial relations or to rewrite the British North America Act would be major positional policies, since they could be interpreted as attempts by some groups to enhance their position *vis-à-vis* others in the political system. Struggles to reform structures in the Canadian legislative system may also be viewed as positional policies and are therefore subject to the same constraints present in the development of any positional policy.

Some Canadian writers conceive of the policy-making process almost exclusively in terms of the executive.[3] This recent attention to the executive-bureaucratic structures of policy-making is a legitimate reaction to the paucity of Canadian literature on policy outputs and on the internal dynamics of policy-making. This approach wastes little energy with institutions which appear to have no major impact on policy while at the same time channelling attention to structures previously ignored. The need for this type of attitude became even more acute with the advent of new policy-making structures in the Canadian political system after Pierre Elliott Trudeau became Prime Minister in 1968.

Unfortunately, the utility of the concept of policy has been diminished by policy analysts who tend to use it when a more precise term would be appropriate. In addition, the executive-bureaucratic structures do not operate in a vacuum. Somehow demands must be channelled into the system, but policy-making models have been unable to accommodate the influence of political culture and such environmental structures as political parties and interest groups. Public policies are shaped by groups and individuals who make claims, legitimate or not, on the political system. Until the policy-making models are equipped to discuss the making of claims and the power configuration of society, then students of legislative systems may be well advised to treat executive decision-making structures as offering only a partial description of policy-making.

Perhaps the most obvious structure ignored by academic policy-making models has been the Canadian Parliament. While textbook authors naturally mention all structures of government, the most comprehensive text, by Van Loon and Whittington, de-emphasizes the significance of Parliament.[4] This may be due to a reluctance to attribute precise influence to particular institutions, and to the fact that the legislature does not readily fit within any one of the currently accepted models.

It is crucial, in our opinion, to reintegrate the study of policy-making and the traditional study of representative institutions. For the purpose of analysis it is unsatisfactory to separate all pre-parliamentary stages of bills and other matters from the parliamentary process. In the nineteenth century Walter Bagehot's conception of the cabinet as the link between the executive and the legislature helped to dispel the tendency to separate the two structures. Today there are multifarious linkages and the idea of two closed system distorts reality. Would-be reformers of the Canadian political system have avoided any approach which would bring Parliament face to face with the executive-bureaucratic structures of government. If the initiation and refining of legislation were conceptualized as part of one analytic system, then the patterns of communication and influence might be more difficult to disentangle but it would accord more with reality. Figure 2 depicts the legislative system as a combination of pre-parliamentary institutions such as the Prime Minister, cabinet, cabinet subject and legislation committees, the Privy Council Office, the drafting office of the Department of Justice and the other departments, plus the normal parliamentary institutions which include the House of Commons, the Senate and parliamentary committees.

The diagram shows the legislative system in a parliamentary setting. The fusion of the legislative and the executive branches of government distinguishes this model from that developed for the investigation of legislative behaviour in the American Congress. As we shall see, legislation is not drafted in Parliament and government policies are rarely determined on the

Figure 2

THE LEGISLATIVE SYSTEM IN A PARLIAMENTARY SETTING

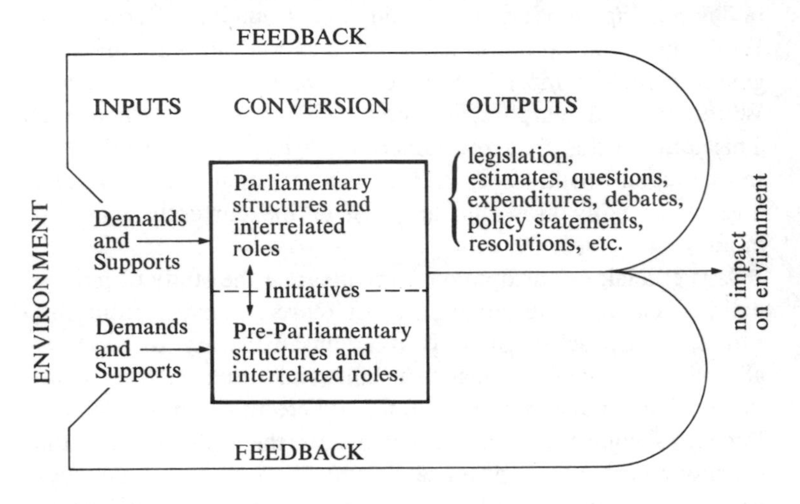

floor of the House of Commons. A series of political and bureaucratic forces are brought to bear on pieces of legislation, the legislative program as a whole, and the schedule for their introduction in the House long before they are actually introduced. If our primary concern is legislation, then it would be a serious mistake to ignore the pre-parliamentary structures. Each structure acts upon legislation at some point. The relation between the pre-parliamentary and the parliamentary structures may be depicted by the word "initiatives." Such initiatives may take the form of bills introduced by the government or resolutions sent from Parliament to the executive, as well as a host of other legal relationships and influence possibilities. The results of these activities (regardless of their origin) are processed through Parliament.

Legislation is perhaps the most obvious output of the system. While an act of Parliament cannot always be distinguished analytically from the general directive of an administrative agency or the decision of a court, it is usually more general and more future-oriented than other modes of authoritative decision-making. Delegated legislation—by which broad statutory authority is given to the executive to formulate regulations—is also an output of the legislative system. Other outputs include expenditure approvals, resolutions and symbolic actions such as questions and debates.

Outputs from the legislative system may or may not have an effect on the environment. Those outputs that do penetrate into the environment help to restructure the schedule of demands and supports for the political system by way of a feedback loop. And, as much as the political system affects the policies which are developed, the content of the outputs helps to structure the nature of the system itself.

While the legislative system approach orients investigations largely in parliamentary terms, not all the tensions outlined in the first chapter deal exclusively with Parliament. In fact, even those which appear to originate in the legislature often deal with relationships between the legislature and other elements in the political system. Because of this, we contend that the resolution of difficulties cannot be satisfactorily accomplished by a reform of isolated structures. The reform of Parliament with little regard for other parts of the system will raise problems even more enigmatic and complex than those which already exist.

FUNCTIONS OF THE LEGISLATIVE SYSTEM

The use of the language of systems analysis in the examination of politics could lead to the conclusion that the legislative system can be understood almost entirely by an appreciation of the external pressures placed upon it and by an examination of system outputs. But from the point of view of reform it is inadequate to conceive of the legislature as a mechanism which simply reacts to environmental influences. The system perspective implies effectiveness and persistence, and yet in some societies the legislative system may be ineffective and fail to survive. On the other hand, some social scientists maintain that the study of legislatures is primarily the study of the behaviour of legislators.[5] This approach concentrates analysis on individual behaviour and gives only minimal consideration to the environment. Neither perspective considers in precise terms the consequences of activity in the legislative system for the political system as a whole.

To organize the discussion of this latter dimension we will

employ the term "function," and suggest several functions that may be performed by the legislative system. In social science the term function has a variety of meanings. It is used here simply to denote the impact which activity in the legislative system may have for the political system. The Canadian legislative system does not differ dramatically from those of other countries. Among the functions attributed to them in the standard literature have been the following: law-making; surveillance; representation; and electoral conversion. Political sociologists have added to this list: recruitment, socialization and training; conflict management; integration; and legitimation.[6] It must be stressed that the legislative system does not enjoy a monopoly on the performance of these functions. Not all those who hold important political offices are recruited through the legislative system nor does the creation of legislation exhaust all law-making. In some countries legislatures do not exist, legislation is not the major expression of law-making, and recruitment and socialization, for example, are carried on by the military and police forces.

The legislative system in Canada performs all of the above functions to some degree, but it is most often associated with the function of law-making. The initiation of bills is practically monopolized by the cabinet and structures in the pre-parliamentary part of the legislative system; parliamentary initiatives normally require cabinet approval or acquiescence. Of course, the formal processing of government-initiated legislation is accomplished in the House of Commons and Senate. Only by the legislative system approach can sense be made of the interrelationships required to perform the law-making function. Moreover, an adequate performance of the law-making function in both parts of the system is necessary for the successful accomplishment of other societal requirements, such as integration and conflict management.[7]

In the study of legislative institutions the term "surveillance" refers to the array of activities undertaken by the legislature in an attempt to supervise and control the executive. The most important of these activities is the examination of the executive's budgetary requirements, but the concept may also be employed to describe such procedures as the supervision of delegated legislation. When the Canadian Parliament reviews the report of the Auditor General it is also performing a surveillance function.

The legislative system performs an important representation function. Few citizens are in close and continuous contact with the political system through their daily lives. Elections are infrequent and individuals seldom choose to participate actively in political parties. The legislative system may provide an access point for individuals whose relationship to the political system would otherwise be tenuous and spasmodic. The member of Parliament is given opportunities to publicly articulate the interests and views of his constituents. Cynics may call some of this activity simply "errand running," but many legislators see this representation function as the central aspect of their role as parliamentarians. It is true, however, that intermediary groups are providing much of the effective representation of national interests. Many political interests are sponsored by interest groups which interact with the executive-bureaucratic structures rather than the legislature. The ability of the legislative system to perform an effective representation function ought to be reassessed in the light of this fact.

In a parliamentary form of government the electoral conversion function should be performed automatically by the legislative system. It involves converting electoral results into general decisions about the composition of cabinets. In Canada the lack of majority party control in the House of Commons and the inability to form coalition governments have often forced political leaders to adopt formal constitutional solutions for essentially political problems.[8] This situation may be dysfunctional for the Canadian political system and may eventually require a reassessment of the electoral laws and perhaps the development of new norms about cabinet composition.

Parliament performs an important activity when it recruits members for other prestigious positions in the political system. The effective performance of this function, and the related activities of training and socialization, are usually aided in other legislatures by a period of apprenticeship and the existence of regular pathways to other roles. Unfortunately, the turnover rate of the Canadian House of Commons hovers around 40 per cent and few individuals have an opportunity to obtain wide experience. Parliament has not always been the recruiting ground for prime ministers, cabinet members or party leaders. Both Prime Minister Trudeau and Robert Stanfield were recruited with almost no experience in the Canadian legislative system. Stanfield walked into the House of Commons as Leader of the Opposition on his first day on Parliament Hill and Trudeau was chosen as Prime Minister of Canada because of his victory at a Liberal party convention.

When the activities of the legislative system produce acquiescence by members of the political system in the moral right of the government to rule, political sociologists say that the legislative system is performing a legitimation function. This function is performed in a manifest manner when the legislature meets to debate and vote on legislative proposals. Unless we appreciate the importance of this function, it is difficult to understand the often lengthy debates, votes and rituals that are brought to bear on initiatives which have been taken elsewhere. In crisis situations such as the FLQ affair of 1970 or disasters such as Hurricane Hazel, the Arrow oil pollution or Manitoba floods, the legislature debated the events only after executive action had been taken. But in each case Parliament legitimized the government's behaviour. The legislature also legitimates government decisions in a latent manner. When the legislature meets ostensibly to perform law-making functions the meeting itself bestows a degree of legitimacy on government.

When legitimation occurs the legislature succeeds in generating support for itself and transferring support to other parts of the political system. These relationships are described as feedback in our model of the legislative system discussed on page 21. The support accorded to the legislative system may be either specific or diffuse. Specific support is the product of favourable attitudes toward those outputs which are responses to specific demands. Diffuse support is a more general and continuous phenomenon best described as a reservoir of good will engendered by the past performance of the system.

To some extent the legislature embodies or symbolizes the

prevailing values in society about how the government should operate. Some of its support comes through the process of political socialization by which attachments are transferred to it from other figures such as the Governor General and the Prime Minister. There is also evidence that the legislature may be a direct "contact point" between the child and the political system.[9] However, rather than viewing the legislature solely as a recipient of support, we believe that it may be able to generate diffuse support for other parts of the political system.[10] This occurs when the legislature enhances the legitimacy of the government, the military, the courts or the bureaucracy. Of course, it should be added that a legislature can detract from legitimacy as well as contribute to it. To perform the legitimation function well, a legislature must obviously command considerable support itself. It is possible that a legislature will even embark on a public relations campaign, as did the Bundestag in modern Germany. The mere existence of the Canadian Parliament is not enough to secure a role for it in the generation or transmittal of support. Parliament must act to protect its own position in the legislative system and especially to ensure that the legitimation function is performed.

NOTES

1. For a summary discussion of the strengths and deficiencies in these models, see Peter Aucoin, "Theory and Research in the Study of Policy-Making," in G. B. Doern and P. Aucoin, eds., *The Structures of Policy-Making in Canada* (Toronto: Macmillan, 1971), pp. 10-38.
2. Theodore Lowi, "American Business, Public Policies, Case Studies, and Political Theory," *World Politics,* Vol. XVI, no. 4 (July 1964), pp. 677-715.
3. See, for example, Doern and Aucoin, eds., *The Structures of Policy-Making.* These authors maintain that "An understanding of how policy is made in the Canadian political system requires that the focus of attention be placed on the executive bureaucratic arena" (p. 267).
4. Richard Van Loon and Michael Whittington, *The Canadian Political System* (Toronto: McGraw-Hill, 1971).
5. The amount of literature in this field can only be described as vast. The seminal work on American legislatures is John Wahlke *et al., The Legislative System* (New York: John

Wiley and Sons, 1962). On Canada, see Allan Kornberg, *Canadian Legislative Behaviour: A Study of the 25th Parliament* (New York: Holt, Rinehart and Winston, 1967).

6. Robert A. Packenham, "Legislatures and Political Development," in Allan Kornberg and Lloyd D. Musolf, eds., *Legislatures in Developmental Perspective* (Durham: Duke University Press, 1970), pp. 521-82, and John D. Lees and Malcolm Shaw, "Committees in Legislatures and the Political System," paper given at International Political Science Association meeting, Montreal, 1973; Murray Edelman, *The Symbolic Uses of Politics* (Urbana: University of Illinois Press, 1964).
7. Two authors advise that the legislative system may collapse if the functions of integration and conflict management are not performed. See Malcolm Jewell and Samuel Patterson, *The Legislative System of the United States* (New York: Random House, 1973).
8. The classic debate over how and when Parliament may be dissolved is one example of how important this problem often is in Canada.
9. David Easton and Jack Dennis, for example, report that near the end of elementary school, children "increasingly tend to see government with Congress at its centre (and) law as its most visible product." *Children in the Political System: Origins of Political Legitimacy* (New York: McGraw-Hill, 1969), p. 120.
10. There is considerable support for this position in the literature on comparative legislatures. See for example, Gerhard Loewenberg, "The Influence of Parliamentary Behaviour on Regime Stability: Some Conceptual Clarifications," *Comparative Politics* 3 (1971), pp. 177-200; and Paul R. Abramson and Ronald Inglehart, "The Development of Systematic Support in Four Western Democracies," *Comparative Political Studies* 2 (1970), pp. 419-42; Loewenberg, "The Institutionalization of Parliament and Public Orientations to the Political System," in Allan Kornberg, *Legislatures in Comparative Perspective,* ed., (New York: David McKay, 1973), pp. 142-156; G. Robert Boynton, Samuel C. Patterson, and Ronald D. Hedlund, "The Structure of Public Support for Legislative Institutions," *Midwest Journal of Political Science* 12 (May 1968), pp. 163-173; Samuel C. Patterson, G. Robert Boynton, and Ronald D. Hedlund, "Perceptions and Expectations of the Legislature and Support for It" *American Journal of Sociology* 75 (July 1969), pp. 62-76.

3. External Influences: The Environment and Structures

The legislative system exists in a complex and changing environment but there are important regularities which help to maintain continuity. As chapter 2 has shown, political scientists have attempted to organize their discussion of the environment by using concepts like demands and supports. The viability of the system is maintained when it reacts to demands in such a manner as to secure support. But these general ideas do not exhaust our appreciation of the environment or its influences. The environment may also be considered in terms of attitudes toward the legislative system, in terms of social and economic resources, and in terms of the issues which dominate political discourse. Our discussion begins with an elaboration of these factors in the Canadian context and then concentrates on structures in the environment, particularly parties and interest groups. While these institutions stand outside the legislative system, they act as intermediaries conveying both demands and supports. Parties and interest groups manifest conflict over issue positions and their continual activity draws together the environment and the legislative system.

POLITICAL CULTURE

The attitudinal dimension of the environment is referred to as political culture. It consists of general public orientations toward the political system and toward government-related activities in the system. The models of governing which Canada inherited from the United States and Britain have fostered certain types of attitudes and behaviour and discouraged others. The most important of these are democratic attitudes toward political participation and governmental authority.

Although the data are limited, they indicate that Canadians

participate very readily in electoral politics.[1] About 75 to 80 per cent of Canadians vote regularly in federal elections. By comparison with many countries, therefore, Canada may be considered to have a "participant" political culture. But the act of voting does not necessarily entail more than passive contact with the political system. Many Canadian citizens who vote regularly take little interest in politics and have a low estimation of their ability to influence political authorities.[2] Only 4 to 5 per cent of the Canadian electorate participate on a continuous basis in political parties or hold elected public office. These individuals usually possess more social, economic and political resources than individuals who participate only passively in the system.

Vested authority and the laws have rarely been questioned in Canadian history.[3] Authority patterns in Canada seem to exhibit a strong element of deference toward political elites. Federal politicians and administrators usually command respect and compliance forces (such as the RCMP and the military) have not been viewed as symbols of oppression as they have in some countries. The Task Force on Government Information found that after indexing responses to two questions on faith in the federal government, only 19 per cent of respondents expressed no confidence on both counts.[4] When asked how often one can trust the government to do what is right, 58 per cent of respondents in both the 1965 and 1968 election studies said "always" or "most of the time."[5] When it came to estimating personal efficacy, only about 25 per cent of Canadians had a low estimation of their capacity to influence governmental authorities.[6] In English Canada deferential attitudes have been traced to the early impact of the United Empire Loyalists, and in French Canada to the strength and flexibility of traditional elites and the lack of commitment to democratic institutions on the part of the mass public. Robert Presthus has examined the literature and data on authority patterns in Canada and adds that deferential attitudes may also result from a combination of monarchical rule, elitist education, pervasive class distinctions and highly bureaucratized institutions.[7]

The combination of passive participation and deference

to authority may be the cornerstone of the attitudes which underlie the viability of the Canadian political system and one reason that strong commitment to ideology is not reflected in the mainstream of political life. In fact, with the exception of the nationalism issues, intense feeling is rarely found. One explanation for the lack of competing ideologies is the presence of a strong liberal philosophy in English Canada and an absolutist tradition in French Canada.[8] The geographic proximity to the United States and the economic dependence on its markets has also provided an impetus for cohesion. Even Canadian literature is permeated by the theme of a persistent struggle for survival.

Conflict and division has not been eliminated from Canadian society. The political culture is not homogeneous and there are several lines of cleavage that occasionally find political expression. Of particular importance are the sometimes hostile relations which prevail between Canada's two charter groups, the French and the English. To some extent ethnic and linguistic divisions have been reinforced by federal arrangements which were designed, in part, to guarantee the persistence of cultural diversity. Immigration policy tended to further reinforce ethnic differences because Canada required large numbers of European immigrants, first to initiate frontier life and later to develop an industrial base.

Regional cleavages have also been prominent in Canadian history. Differences in economic status have combined with regional loyalties to produce a society of rich and poor provinces divided over the type and extent of central government interference required in the economy. Recent findings indicate significant regional differences in levels of trust, efficacy and involvement which suggest the existence of regional political cultures.[9] These cleavages seem to have diminished prospects for class conflict in Canada, but there remains a possibility that the Canadian political culture will eventually be considerably more affected by the process of industrialization.

The cohesion found in the Canadian political culture has been strong enough to permit division and conflict without the eruption of widespread violence. This has meant that while societal cleavages constantly threaten the country, politicians can rely on deep-seated attitudes to maintain the independence and authority of the legislative system. Canadian modes of participation and attitudes toward authority have generated at least enough support to permit politicians to make piecemeal adjustments in public policy in response to specific demands.

SOCIAL AND ECONOMIC DETERMINANTS

When the environment is viewed primarily in terms of political culture it is difficult to assess its precise impact on the legislative system. In an attempt to resolve this problem, some policy analysts have developed concepts and statistics to show the relations between the socio-economic context of a nation and its policy output. This methodology requires the use of quantifiable variables such as per capita income, age distribution of the population and level of industrialization as "environmental" indicators. For the most part "policy output" is defined very generally as whatever the government does, and much of the data used is output from the legislative system, namely legislation. By finding indicators for each of these types of variables and by systematically performing correlations, researchers have isolated those variables which have a significant, independent effect on policy output.

In such studies the impact of political variables (such as legislative apportionment and type of party system) on public policy is usually found to be insignificant. Instead, the system's social and economic characteristics are found to have the greatest impact on policy output. At the extreme, some researchers, interested in American state politics, claim that environmental factors can account for most public policy and that politicians and legislatures have very little, if any, effect on the outputs of the political system.[10] In Canada the analyses of public policy have also yielded unflattering results for the importance of political variables. A comprehensive study of twenty-seven Canadian parliaments has indicated that there is a strong direct link between environmental factors and public policy. But characteristics of the Canadian legislative elite and aspects of political change (political variables) have little independent relation to policy output.[11]

Despite its appeal, this approach has not provided a satisfactory answer to some important questions about the relationships among environmental factors, the legislative system and policy outputs. While environmenal factors are obviously significant for public policy, it is difficult to find, quantify, and especially weight most environmental variables. Similarly, the political variables chosen do not always seem appropriate. None of these models provide for the dynamism found in politics and not all take into consideration the impact of the legislative system on particular types of policies. Furthermore, even among technicians in this field there is agreement that much of the variance remains to be accounted for statistically. It is this unexplained variance which is most important to political scientists. Even if policy analysts were to claim that Canada's unemployment insurance policies are environmentally determined (i.e., the level of GNP indicates that the country will have such a policy), its details may not be, and these details may alter attitudes toward all of the unemployment policy, and possibly aid in producing a new one. Gross data analysis does not (and without extensive refinement cannot) account for the choices made among policies, amendments to legislation, or the timing of legislative outputs. And these are policy-making and legislative roles which politicians consider important and which students of legislatures cannot ignore.

POLITICAL ISSUES

The environment, defined either as political culture or as the social and economic context of society, places constraints on public policy-making and hence on the substantive outputs of the legislative system. Political authorities cannot dispose of resources they do not have, nor can they afford to consistently violate patterns of behaviour which are valued by the mass public. When major problems are confronted, environmental factors limit the number of policy alternatives available to politicians. Ideally, it is the politician's role to transform the demands which emerge from the environment into debatable issues, to outline the alternatives, and to endorse a course of action. In this way, politicians can claim a unique role in the political system.

Recent Canadian examples illustrate the emergence of issues

from the environment. The ethnic-linguistic cleavage has produced questions such as whether or not the province of Quebec should be allowed to separate and the degree to which the federal public service and other federal bodies should consist of bilingual personnel. Emerging from regional cleavages have been issues such as agricultural subsidies, differential tariffs and the distribution of oil revenues. Cleavages are not always the source of problems but they usually aggravate them. The Roman Catholic–Protestant cleavage has complicated the abortion issue in Canada and since 1969 federal politicians have been reluctant to permit an open debate in Parliament. Such issues have created tensions in political parties and given rise to significant demands on the legislative system.

INTEREST GROUPS

Implicit in the argument that the environment is the source of issue possibilities for the legislative system is the idea that means exist to convey these issues in the form of demands to political authorities in the system. Those structures which exist to transmit these inputs must be compatible with the political culture. In Canada interest groups generally meet this requirement. They are successful in marshalling support for issues and providing ideas for public policy without displacing the decision-makers themselves. Their activities assist the legislative system to perform the multitude of functions ascribed to it. It has even been suggested that the Canadian political culture contains an organic view of society which nurtures the corporatist idea that the most important interactions in the political system *ought* to transpire between major social groupings.[12]

Beyond the fact that interest group activity is an accepted part of the political system, three basic facts about group life in Canada need to be mentioned. First, there are many different types of interest groups with different resources, tactics and goals. They range from promotional groups such as the Canadian Temperance Society through to self-interested groups such as the Canadian Manufacturers' Association; from groups active in the legislative system, such as the Canadian Labour Congress through to those like the Canadian Institute of Nursing whose connection with the legislative system is at most transient. The differences among interest groups have repercussions in the political system primarily because they seem to have a strong influence on the success or failure of group objectives.

The second general point is that the interaction between interest group leaders (and lobbyists), bureaucrats and politicians is permeated by the ethos of mutual accommodation. This means that the interaction involving interest groups in the political system is characterized by cooperation in which each party is considered by the others to have a legitimate share in the making of public policy. The accommodation depends upon all parties receiving enough satisfaction that continued interaction is deemed worthwhile. Nowhere is the phenomenon of mutual accommodation more apparent than in clientele relations established between interest groups and government departments. Examples include the close affinity developed between the Canadian Federation of Mayors and Municipalities and the Ministry of Housing and Urban Affairs, or between the Canadian Legion and the Department of Veterans' Affairs.

Thirdly, the legislative system is not the only focus of interest group activity. Interest groups often devote a great deal of time to decisions of an administrative nature. It is sometimes more important and often easier to affect the substance of a policy at the earliest stages of policy formulation or at the stage of its implementation rather than in the legislative system. This is one reason for the frequent criticism that interest group leaders by-pass Parliament in their attempts to influence policy.

When groups do attempt to influence decisions in the legislative system, access to decision-makers at important stages becomes a necessary condition of success. The existence of an access point is not a guarantee of influence, but without access almost nothing else is possible. Of equal importance is the fact that access is heavily influenced by the institutional and procedural structure of the legislative system. Initially, influence may depend upon the extent to which groups are able to participate in the politics of mutual accommodation. Beyond this, groups must succeed in adapting to the legislative system and using the access points provided.

Successful access to bureaucrats and politicians hinges in part, on the type of group, its status, and its organizational resources, such as membership size, finances and the quality of its personnel. According to Robert Presthus, religious, educational and business groups seek access primarily through the cabinet, welfare groups through the bureaucracy, and labour through the legislature.[13] Given their styles and resources, groups are attracted to particular parts of the legislative system on a semi-continuous basis. This tendency is accentuated by the fact that certain policies receive consideration primarily in one arena. Groups interested in obtaining a continuation of Local Initiatives Projects, for example, have concentrated more attention on the pre-parliamentary part of the legislative system. Parliament, on the other hand, has more attraction for those groups interested in pursuing such topics as the abolition of hanging and the reform of abortion laws.

There are a limited number of access points and few groups can afford to continually ignore any possibilities for influence. It is only the most marginal and violent of groups which fail to adapt to the access points available in the legislative system. Eventually, interest groups employ every tactic and approach every available target of influence. Among the tactics used are personal representations to members of the legislative system, public relations activities, the enlisting of membership for mail campaigns, and the presentation of briefs containing expert opinions and information. The stress on particular tactics depends largely on the group's resources and the types of issues involved. As a tactic, for example, personal representation or lobbying is most often employed by business groups in Canada while the enlisting of membership support is a tactic employed by professional groups such as the Canadian Medical Association.

In the pre-parliamentary stages of the legislative system the norms of secrecy influence the style and content of interactions. Even when a policy has been agreed upon, groups are not always made aware of the decision or the policy details. All ministers may be vaguely aware of an interest group demand, but only the minister responsible and perhaps one or two with strong regional or constituency interests will even read (or have their officials read) the letters and briefs which are sent by interest groups. Interest group representatives are not informed of the content of cabinet decisions or given the text of a bill before it is introduced in the House of Commons. In the pre-parliamentary stages of the process cabinet takes the position that the minister responsible for a new policy should give an audience to interested parties. Groups may be requested to provide information or advice on the subject area without being advised of the exact nature of the government's intentions. Such an atmosphere allows ministers and senior public servants to achieve some independence from interest groups and permits the cabinet to act as a collective decision-making body.

These characteristics of the legislative system stifle access, but others tend to break down this atmosphere. Public servants, among others, cannot afford to alienate interest groups on whom they depend for some of the expert opinions they provide their ministers. Also, the mere fact that legislation, as we will discuss more fully, is often returned to departments for reconsideration results in an opening up of the process. It means that consultation must resume and that groups which wish to block proposals may have further opportunities to lobby bureaucrats. For example, groups which lobbied against the government's initial proposals for a new tax system in the late 1960s were given, and took, every opportunity afforded in the legislative system to raise objections. Interest groups are not always concerned with blocking proposals, but the complexities of the legislative system and the rough landscape of Canadian politics give some indication of why it is generally considered easier to block or slow down proposals than to initiate them.

By the time it enters the parliamentary part of the system, legislation has usually undergone a significant input from interest groups. The views of most groups have been given a hearing. At this stage policy is well formed, but it is not irreversible. Interest groups which have been unable to secure access to the cabinet or the bureaucracy, or have been unsatisfied with the results of consultation, often find that more than one opportunity exists to influence the passage of legislation in Parliament. Caucus, the meeting of the parliamentary party, usually affords the first opportunity. Before a bill is introduced in the House an outline of the new policy direction is given to the government caucus. At the weekly meetings which follow, caucus members are given opportunities to express the sentiments and grievances of interest groups. Even when the bill has been introduced for first reading in the House, caucus continues to debate the bill and sometimes prevents the moving of second reading.

When bills are before the House a multitude of devices exist for retarding their progress. Many of these procedures are too complicated for the public to gain much of an appreciation of what has actually transpired in Parliament. Moreover, the passage of legislation is often a lengthy process and only the most devoted Parliament-watcher can follow the machinations of politicians as they manoeuvre to escape the wrath of major interest groups. The controversial Drug Bill was first introduced in the House in 1962 but did not secure passage until 1968. By that time its contents were well known, two governments had been in power and interest groups had been given extensive opportunities to renew lobbying activities and conduct public relations campaigns. In the case of the new tax bill, the process began with Mr. Diefenbaker's decision to set up the Carter Commission in 1962, and the bill did not receive final approval until 1972. The last-minute amendment which favoured the cooperatives was the direct result of interest group pressure combined with provincial support, backbench approval, and the government's desire either to prevent a showdown or be conciliatory in order to get the bill through the committee stage. Interest groups are given added opportunities for access when the government prolongs the process by introducing legislation, like the Competitions Act of 1972, for the prime purpose of having its contents subjected to interest group criticism. This tactic sometimes amounts to little more than a manipulation of the legislative system to help solve policy difficulties in the governing party.

In the parliamentary part of the system interest groups may lobby members of Parliament individually or they may seek to publicize their views before the committee system of the House of Commons. In either case, the efforts often appear hopeless. On his own the individual member is usually of little consequence unless he commands special knowledge or is in a tense minority government situation. Nevertheless, interest group leaders continue to discuss policy issues with members of Parliament. One of the main reasons is that cabinet members are, to some degree, recruited from the ranks of the government backbench and neither they nor opposition members can be made to feel isolated or ignored. Both groups have significant potential influence. Members may also become good public relations agents for various interests. Although most members do not acknowledge much interest group influence in their own elections, there are strong possibilities for group activity in those constituencies where group interests are concentrated. But the major reason for constant group pressure on the backbench may be the belief that a changed opinion there may force an alteration in cabinet's position. Generally cabinet opinion prevails when the caucus, the provinces, or the relevant interest groups can be attracted to cabinet's side. Cabinet has the least chance of imposing its views when all three of these elements resist its direction. Major interest groups will therefore attempt to affect a coalition of at least some anti-government forces, the backbench included, in cases where cabinet and interest group opinion diverge. In minority situations, opposition attitudes become another element weighing heavily in the equation and demanding interest group attention.

Legislators seem to regard the committee system as the most important forum of interest group influence in Parliament.[14] It is attractive from the interest group point of view because individuals with different perspectives are assembled for the primary purpose of listening to and commenting upon interest group arguments. Committee meetings afford an opportunity to present briefs to the government and obtain at least limited publicity for interest group endeavours.

It is clear, however, that lobbying both the individual legislator and the committee system represent long-term interest group investment. In majority governments and even in minority situations, individual legislators are unable to alter dramatically the course of public policy. Throughout the legislative system responsibility and control of legislation rests in the hands of the government. The Canadian Parliament, as we have already suggested, does not make laws, it passes them. Policies, bills and expenditures are at least partially woven together and it is difficult for cabinet to permit adjustment of single policies or bills without destroying the delicate compromises that have been made in the whole legislative program. Furthermore, legislators and committees rarely act on policies soon enough.

The mutual accommodation which prevails between interest groups and actors in the political system can now be further elaborated. Interest groups offer to political actors invaluable information about the state of the political environment. They also make it possible for politicians and bureaucrats to understand the environment by communicating consolidated attitudes. Information costs are thus diminished for the system. In recent years the Department of Agriculture, for example, has been encouraging farmers to unite under the umbrella of one organization primarily for this purpose. Interest groups provide a reservoir of expert skills which can be made available to government. Of some importance also is the actual personnel which groups provide to the legislative system, usually to the bureaucracy but sometimes to Parliament and the cabinet.

Participation in the legislative system provides interest groups with two major advantages. First, it provides several discrete points of access to one part of the policy-making process, a benefit which enables interest group leaders to claim that they are succeeding in pressing for their groups' interests. Not only is this a necessary consideration for goal attainment, but interaction within the system serves as a bulwark against threats to the organization. When interest groups use points of access they can rely upon established patterns of consultation, the frequent support of public servants and a reasonable degree of privacy in their interactions.

The second major benefit is perhaps more abstract. Interest

groups are often able to obtain legitimacy by their interactions within the legislative system.[15] Legitimacy may be thought of as the quality of moral acceptability which is believed to accompany political action. To be able to influence the course of both policy formation and its application interest groups must have legitimate claims to make and be considered legitimate vehicles for the expression of such claims. Interaction within the legislative system permits interest groups to obtain a high degree of legitimacy. Thus cabinet, by hearing annual representations from such large interest groups as the Canadian Labour Congress and the Canadian Chamber of Commerce and by considering their briefs, is able to accord some degree of legitimacy to their goals and methods of attaining them. However, legitimacy is also a quality traceable to societal standards. It is possible for the cabinet, the bureaucracy or the legislature to confer legitimacy upon the activities of groups only if the goals and tactics of the group are compatible with standards present in Canadian political culture. Thus, rival groups compete for recognition to enhance their legitimacy but the nature of some groups, such as the FLQ, makes their recognition in the legislative system highly unlikely.

The general problems in the legislative system, discussed in chapter one, are aggravated by certain aspects of interest group activity. Representation, and hence participation in the Canadian legislative system, is supposed to be achieved through the electoral process which is founded on a somewhat ambivalent application of the one man, one vote principle.[16] However, this form of representation, which is based on the views of individual constituents, has been replaced to some degree by what can be called "functional representation." According to this perspective interest groups constitute a major legitimate form of political representation. It is argued, implicitly, that groups are perhaps the most important interests deserving of representation and that the constituency form of representation is unable to meet the demands of groups in the political system. Furthermore, the requirements of a modern welfare state make the representation of interest groups a necessary adjunct to government activity. Without the eventual cooperation of doctors, for example, the Canadian government would probably have failed in imposing medicare. In Canada, the increasingly high ratio of government expenditure to GNP may make cooperation an even more common requirement in the future.

The advocacy of functional representation depends on an exalted view of the role groups ought to play in the formation of public policy. The proliferation of advisory councils attached to government departments, such as the Canadian Welfare Council and the Canadian Consumer Council, is one indication of the appeal of this type of representation. The implications for democratic accountability are clear. The drainage of public authority to interest groups, which is implied in this notion of representation, erodes political responsibility in a representative democracy.

It may be that members of Parliament were never able to represent constituents in anything but the Burkean fashion with its emphasis on independent judgment. But if representation is also to mean the offering of broad policy guidelines, then even here interest groups, or advisory committees attached to departments, are presently offering a significant proportion of the information and the arguments. As long as arrangements exist to accommodate such policy advice from interest groups, then there is strong justification for demanding that elected representatives be given more opportunities to affect the content of public policy.

It has already been mentioned that groups differ substantially in their style, tactics and resources. Groups with large operating budgets and a prestigious membership, for example, seem to possess a greater means of achieving and maintaining access in most situations. No simple correlation exists between resources and success, but most observers have found at least some relationship. However, structure and resources are not the only conditions of effective access. As shown above, interest groups must also succeed in identifying their own goals with dominant values in the political culture. In Canada organized labour has not had the success in this regard which it seems to have achieved in Britain and the United States. To some degree its goals stand outside the dominant belief system and this is reinforced by the existence of close relations between labour and the NDP which has been unable to achieve power at the federal level. In Canada labour does not constitute the electoral threat it does in Britain, nor has it been identified with a major party as in the United States.

Unlike other groups which suffer a lack of legitimacy, labour organizations have tried to adjust to the accepted norms of interaction in the legislative system. On the other hand, some organizations have employed tactics which violate accepted norms. For example, the government cancelled Local Initiative Projects for groups which publicly demonstrated to have their grants extended. The norms of mutual accommodation exclude the type of ultimatum conveyed by demonstrations. In Canada the standard practice is negotiation of individual group claims, a rule which is violated at a group's peril. Thus, the legislative system demonstrates a certain rigidity in interest group relations.

The most obvious example of this rigidity can be found in the lack of response to the unorganized. Along with other largely unorganized interests in society, consumers and old age pensioners do not possess the resources to sustain mass organization. Decisions such as those to lower the drinking age or to raise annual income supplements for the elderly are often made in the absence of pressure from those directly affected. So complete is the spirit of accommodation and consultation among organized groups that the unorganized are placed at an overwhelming disadvantage. The institutions of the legislature system should be developed to respond to this challenge.

POLITICAL PARTIES

The difficulties which attend group politics may be resolved by the activities of political parties. While interest groups enjoy pervasive influence they are usually unable to overcome their narrow interests or to articulate all the demands of a society. According to classical democratic theory, political parties, by their role in elections, are supposed to respond to such deficiencies in the articulation and aggregation of societal demands.[17] In Canada, however, political parties have achieved only partial success in ameliorating the problems created by our system of interest group politics.[18]

Political parties are organized to contest elections for the attainment of political office and the realization of generalized goals. Such purposes require a specificity of roles and structures. In Canada the activities of all four political parties which contest federal elections are based on a relatively small membership core. The Liberal, Progressive Conservative and Social Credit parties rely on the direct participation of committed party workers. The New Democratic Party similarly depends on a membership core, although it can claim the indirect membership of union affiliates. In all parties the relationships between constituency, provincial and federal structures, are more weakly articulated than in the United Kingdom. The lines of communication between the components are intermittent except during election campaigns. With the exception of the NDP, whose workers are more inclined to participate at both the federal and provincial levels, party organization in Canada is strongly influenced by the federal system of government. Provincial units are not inferior wings of the party and many party members are content to pursue political careers at only one level of the political system. By defending either provincial or federal interests the party leaders are occasionally required to assume opposing policy positions.

In addition to being decentralized Canadian political parties must face electors whose psychological identification with particular parties appears to be volatile. For example, a significant proportion of Canadian voters support one party at the provincial level and another at the national level. Despite this there is continuity in the electoral process with few dramatic reversals in national voting trends. Only the Progressive Conservatives and the Liberals have ever held federal office in Canada, while neither the New Democratic nor the Social Credit parties have ever received more than one quarter of the votes cast in a federal election.

Political parties should be able to accomplish at least three basic tasks for the legislative system: aggregate demands from society, provide decision-makers, and offer practical and systematic policy contributions on a continuing basis.

Parties are "gatekeepers" in the political system, channelling some demands directly to decision-makers, and eliminating and combining others. Electoral success in Canada has depended on an efficient performance of this function. The Conservatives and Liberals have achieved office primarily by forging a broad coalition of interests, particularly ethnic and regional. In the employment of this strategy these parties have contributed to political integration. Furthermore, success in interest aggregation has permitted the Liberals and Conservatives to provide managers and decision-makers for the legislative system. Cabinet composition, with its emphasis on regional representation, also symbolizes a compromise of interests. On the other hand, parties which have attempted to capture public office with a program based on a single principle or ideology have been unsuccessful either in aggregating interests or in providing decision-makers. In recent years even the New Democratic Party has been prepared to vitiate its program in the pursuit of national office, a strategy which illustrates the fundamental importance of interest aggregation for electoral success in Canada.

There are limitations on the extent to which political parties may have an independent policy-making role and make major policy contributions in the legislative system. A party program, at minimum, is a set of coordinated and consistent policies designed to achieve goals with which the parties are identified. Only the NDP and Social Credit have had even moderate success in generating such programs. The fact that the two major political parties do not have distinguishable programs means it is difficult for either of them to insist on the resolution of issues according to the dictates of party principle. The aggregation function that the Liberals and Conservatives perform so singlemindedly impedes the development of comparable programs. Parties that attempt to mediate diverse and sometimes inconsistent demands in order to achieve electoral victory cannot afford the rigidity firm policy commitments imply.

It may be argued that even though political leaders are primarily conscious of winning elections, this need not interfere with the party's role as an agent of policy development. Elected representatives, according to this view, are held accountable in a democracy by elections in which their policies are confirmed or rejected. However, electoral research has indicated that voters have considerable difficulty distinguishing among the contesting parties on matters of policy. The parties are, therefore, unable to extract clear policy directives out of election results. Elections are rarely a source of policy communication and political parties cannot transform general feelings into specific policy alternatives which are the substance of the legislative system. Individual parties cannot claim, even with an electoral majority, that the votes cast on their behalf illustrate the electorate's commitment to one or all of their policies. This fact does not mean that issues are not discussed or ideas developed for election campaigns. Politicians design policies to cater to imperfect notions of electoral attitudes and many policies are constructed in a random fashion during the frenzy of election campaigning. In the 1972 general election both the Conservatives and the Liberals scrambled to respond to the "corporate rip-off" issue pressed by the New Democrats. In the 1974 election it was the NDP and the Liberals who were forced to organize their campaign in reaction to the Conservative "wage and price freeze." None of the major parties appear committed to substituting a programmatic approach for the present pattern of electoral campaigning.

Do party organizations in Canada act as policy stimulants between elections? The answer is mixed. The acknowledged role of the party organization in Canada is to achieve the party's electoral victory. Workers and organizers seem to demonstrate more concern over their party's slogans than over its policies. Part of the reason lies in the importance of the electoral battle from the participants' point of view. The emphasis parties place on electoral victory complements the attitudes of many party workers who display little interest in politics except during the excitement of election campaigns.

Canadian parties recognize that their members are not primarily concerned with policy questions. They provide infrequent opportunities for members to contribute to policy formation. All parties have been experimenting with periodic policy conventions in recent years (the NDP bi-annually and the Conservatives and Liberals every two to four years) but their impact on the party leadership is uncertain. The relatively high degree of intra-party democracy which these conventions demonstrate cannot be equated with a significant policy input. The status of convention policy statements is ambiguous, even in the NDP. There is an unmistakable feeling on the part of rank and file members in the governing party that the cabinet politely entertains the policy ideas of the party organization, but expends most of its energy attempting to avoid embarrassing inconsistencies in party and government policy. This is a matter for interpretation. In the 1968 Liberal government, Trudeau initiated the practice of appending Liberal convention resolutions to every cabinet document. Ministers were, therefore, always made aware of the relationship between party positions and government decisions. Cabinet debate sometimes centred on the discrepancies and on occasion attempts were made to reconcile conflicting views. This meant that some convention issues received a second hearing in the inner circles of government. It did not mean, however, that all convention resolutions were discussed by cabinet.

From the point of view of the party as an organization, policy is perhaps best conceived as an instrument rather than a goal. The party must have a policy if it is to mobilize electoral support, and some policies are designed to do little more. On most occasions the so-called Thinkers' Conferences have also been used for this purpose. In recent decades the Conservative party has clambered over the obstacles of French nationalism in its search for policies with which to attract the Quebec electorate, while the Liberals have sought policies with which to appease the West. Policies may also be used to sanctify political positions which are adopted for pragmatic purposes. The fact that the party organization tends to follow rather than lead makes this tactic an easy and convenient one. Finally, policy may be used to recruit new personnel into the party organization. Although party activists tend to continue their participation for social and personal reasons, the initial participation of many members is often prompted by policy considerations of a very general nature.[19] Politicians cannot afford to adopt policies which might alienate large numbers of weak identifiers or individuals who occasionally lend active support to the party.

In the legislative system itself the bureaucracy tends to exercise a modifying effect on those policies which do emerge from the mass party organization and the electoral battle. The party *qua* government inherits a public service which advised its predecessor and seems inexhaustably capable of offering objections, financial or technical, to proposals whose merits seemed quite obvious in party circles. Added to this is the basically incremental nature of public policy formation in Canada. New policies, as we have mentioned, tend to emerge out of the old ones and party policies are often not attuned to this fact.

Since Canadian political parties are not well organized for the task of policy formation, it would seem that they should have little influence in the legislative system. However, the influence of political parties seems to be ubiquitous. The most independent of politicians and the most disinterested of bureaucrats must, on occasion, take into consideration the views of parties. However, it is not the mass party which has much influence but the senior officers of the central party organization and the members of the parliamentary party. At high political levels the overlap of personnel, access, and self-interest in party success necessitates close liaison.

Under Trudeau formal arrangements have been established to provide a continual dialogue between the government and the Liberal party. Regular meetings are held between PMO staff, the president of the Liberal Federation, and the Parliamentary Secretary to the Prime Minister. Regional officers link the Prime Minister and PMO to party organizations and group interests through the country. Perhaps the most important expression of party influence is the operation of "troikas" which consist of the senior minister from a region, a member of the parliamentary party, and a nominee of the Liberal Federation. In concert these individuals exercise some authority where the government has discretionary powers to make appointments, select contractors, or affect strictly regional changes.

Senior party officials meet with cabinet members and caucus

on a semi-regular basis. In the Progressive Conservative party, the national director is continually invited to meetings with Robert Stanfield and occasionally attends caucus. Since 1970 the Liberal party has organized a "political cabinet," which is a special meeting of cabinet usually attended by party officials. While political cabinet was developed primarily for campaign purposes, the congruence of government policy and campaign interests is also determined in these meetings. The Election Expenses bill, 1971–72 vintage, was discussed in detail with at least one financial officer of the National Liberal Party Federation. The national director has, on occasion, attended formal cabinet committee meetings to discuss policy matters, and the schedule of legislative proposals has been amended on his initiative. Senior party officials may therefore find themselves actually taking part in cabinet policy-making.

The majority party exercises another form of control over policy because of the nature of the parliamentary system. In Canada the private meeting of each parliamentary party is referred to as caucus. The support of the government caucus is crucial for cabinet survival. While not a policy initiator caucus does exercise a broad control over the government's policies and legislative program. As a body, it must occasionally be appeased. The parliamentary party is afforded opportunities to discuss almost all policy matters before they are discussed in the House of Commons. In 1972, for example, the Liberal party caucus alone prevented the government from moving second reading of an amendment to the British North America Act which would have altered electoral distribution and caused Quebec members some embarrassment in their own province. The formula for backbench success in this regard is the same as that for interest groups; if a coalition of provincial, group and backbench interests can be formed then the cabinet's power to command adherence to its policies is severely limited.

Canadian parliamentary parties cannot always be considered consensual bodies of opinion on policy. By comparison with the British Conservative party's "Monday Group" and Labour's "Pro-Common Market Group," Canadian parties have not experienced the type of backbench dissension necessary to maintain full-fledged factions, but there are "tendencies" in all parties. Several reasons exist. The major parties, as we have mentioned, are aggregating parties, and, as a result, the issues with which they identify are diverse and therefore provide much scope for criticism. The regional nature of many political issues in Canada, and the regional nature of political representation occasionally force the cabinet to assuage certain backbench policy tendencies. But internal conflict over policy is even more apparent in programmatic parties. Both the NDP and the Social Credit party have experienced considerable dissension on policy issues.

The nature of the legislative system may also affect harmony on policy matters. The norms of cabinet secrecy mean that the cabinet may take government backbenchers into its confidence on policy issues only after the major decisions have been taken. Yet cabinet seems to recognize that it is an advantage to have backbench opinion channelled into cabinet discussions as early as possible in the policy-making process and recent changes in caucus organization have attempted to achieve some measure of backbench influence. With such procedures cabinet can take advantage of its own secret operations to determine which policy path will avoid conflict among its supporters. Whether the new communication links will actually yield benefits, either for cabinet control or backbench influence, also depends on the effectiveness of other organizations. It is well known that the Trudeau government improved communication between the government bureaucracy and the cabinet by strengthening the Privy Council Office. But PCO has been purposely excluded from open interaction with such obviously "political" bodies as caucus. It was perhaps envisaged that an expanded PMO would provide the necessary liaison. But its activity suggests that it is more likely to have an affinity with PCO than with party stalwarts in the House of Commons.

The ineffectiveness of mass party control over policy formation is demonstrable but, as we have shown, many opportunities exist for senior party bureaucrats and backbenchers to be involved in policy-making. When interest group pressures provincial concern and backbench intransigence combine there is a likclihood of government appeasement either on the policy itself or, more likely, on the timing of its implementation. The inner circle may be the apex of decision-making in Canada, but its policy options are narrowed as it attempts to reconcile the limitations of finance, the demands of cultural norms, and the claims of provinces, groups, party bureaucrats and caucus. Nevertheless, when the Prime Minister can develop a consistency in his policies and legislative activities, the weapons at the disposal of the inner circle are formidable.

NOTES

1. Rick Van Loon, "Political Participation in Canada: The 1965 Election," *Canadian Journal of Political Science,* Vol. III, no. 3 (September 1970), pp. 376-399.
2. Ibid., pp. 393-396.
3. See, for example, Seymour Martin Lipset, "Revolution and Counter-Revolution: The United States and Canada," in O. Kruhlak, R. Shultz, and S. Pobihushchy, eds., *The Canadian Political Process* (Toronto: Holt, Rinehart and Winston, 1970), pp. 13-38.
4. *Task Force on Government Information,* Vol. II (Ottawa: Queen's Printer, 1969), p. 70.
5. Reported in Robert Presthus, *Elite Accommodation in Canadian Politics* (Toronto: Macmillan of Canada, 1973), p. 45.
6. Adapted from Van Loon, "Political Participation," p. 393.
7. Presthus, *Elite Accommodation,* p. 29.
8. Kenneth D. McRae, "The Structure of Canadian History," in Louis Hartz, ed., *The Founding of New Societies* (New York: Harcourt, Brace and World, 1964), pp. 219-272.
9. Richard Simeon and David J. Elkins, "Regional Political Cultures in Canada," unpublished paper, 1974.
10. The literature in this field has been summarized in J. Fenton and D. W. Chamberlayne, "The Literature Dealing with the Relationship between Political Processes, Socio-Economic Conditions and the Public Policies in the American States: A Bibliographic Essay, *Polity,* Vol. 2 (Spring 1969), pp. 388-394. See also T. R. Dye, *Politics, Economics and the Public: Policy Outcomes in the American States* (Chicago: Rand McNally, 1966), and I. Sharkansky and R. Hofferbert, "Dimensions of State Politics, Economics and Public Policy, "*American Political Science Review,* Vol. 63, no. 4 (December 1969), pp. 868-879.

11. Allan Kornberg, David Falcone, William T. E. Mishler, II, *Legislatures and Societal Change: The Case of Canada* (Beverly Hills: Sage Publications, 1973).
12. Presthus, *Elite Accommodation*, pp. 28-37.
13. Ibid., Chapter 6. It should be noted that Presthus' data were collected in the provinces as well as at the federal level, and frequently the data are presented without these distinctions.
14. Robert Presthus, "Interest Groups and the Canadian Parliament: Activities, Interaction, Legitimacy and Influence," *Canadian Journal of Political Science*, Vol. IV, no. 4 (December 1971), p. 452.
15. For an extended discussion of legitimacy and related concepts, see David Kwavnick, *Organized Labour and Pressure Politics* (Montreal: McGill-Queen's University Press, 1972), Chapter 1.
16. T. H. Qualter, *The Election Process in Canada* (Toronto: McGraw-Hill, 1970), Chapter 3.
17. H. B. Mayo, *Introduction to Democratic Theory* (New York: Oxford University Press, 1960).
18. On some of the problems faced by Canadian political parties, see John Meisel, "Recent Changes in Canadian Political Parties," in Hugh Thorburn, ed., *Party Politics in Canada,* 2nd ed. (Scarborough, Ont.: Prentice-Hall, 1967), pp. 33-54.
19. There are no published studies in Canada, but much research has been done in the United States. See, for example, James Q. Wilson, *The Amateur Democrat* (Chicago: University of Chicago Press, 1962).

4. The Inner Circle

THE CONTEXT OF POLICY AND LEGISLATION

In a democracy institutions are established to convert societal demands into satisfactory political outputs. From the Prime Minister to the smallest municipal office holder, there are individuals prepared to assume leadership roles in every Canadian institution. This chapter is devoted to an examination of those institutions and individuals responsible for sorting out demands and setting priorities at the national level. In our parliamentary form of government the constitution provides for the fusion of executive and legislative powers by requiring overlapping membership in the cabinet and Parliament. This type of fusion centralizes governmental authority in the hands of any individual or group who can maintain the loyalty or acquiescence of a majority of Canada's elected representatives. Buttressed by mass party organizations and a permanent public service, the Prime Minister, his cabinet, and senior officials have acquired the responsibility for authoritative decision-making and the power to behave as an inner circle in the Canadian legislative system.[1]

These facts have provided the foundation for arguments that Canada has developed a prime ministerial government,[2] led by an all-powerful "super group" somehow out of step with the requirements of parliamentary democracy. This complex question has too often suffered from superficial treatment.[3] In Canada's composite government influence and power are widely dispersed throughout the country and conflict is inherent in the major policy-making institutions. Within the legislative system a constant exchange of opinions and sentiments occurs between actors in the pre-parliamentary and the parliamentary sectors. As we will see in this and later chapters, the Prime Minister cannot exercise personal power in Parliament independent of the views of either his supporters or his antagonists. Not even in the inner circle can he hope to be effective if he fails to anticipate the reactions of his closest colleagues. On substantive issues he and his advisors must guide the cabinet toward a policy path which avoids a coalition of hostile interests capable of blocking government initiatives. No prime minister (or super group) can embark on a new policy direction without securing the loyalty of his followers and anticipating obstacles in both parts of the legislative system.

Discussion about the existence of prime ministerial government in Canada is confused by arguments about the location of power in the political system. While decision-making theorists have discarded the idea that a "lump of power" exists anywhere, Canadian commentators persist in using the concept of power in this unique spacial manner. The Prime Minister's power, however, is not like currency: it cannot be located spacially or spent conceptually. Power ought to be employed as a relational concept which links together two or more actors, with different political resources, in a situation involving a multitude of influences, including severe losses for noncompliance.[4] When academics have examined the evolution of individual bills for power configurations, for example, they have always found that a myriad of influences were at work, including phenomena as disparate as political culture and the idiosyncracies of individual members of Parliament. Very seldom has the threat of severe losses been shown to be included in the member's equation, and, therefore, the concept of power has little utility. Moreover, comparing the power of individuals requires insuring that situations are comparable. This is a complex but indispensable task which few Canadian commentators have been inclined to undertake. The great Canadian debate about whether or not Trudeau inaugurated prime ministerial government in 1968 owes as much to a journalistic conception of power, as it does to some misunderstandings about the detailed relations among the parts of the legislative system.

The political resources of the Prime Minister and the executive are undeniably extensive. The constitutional prerogatives of the executive to introduce legislation, spend money and make appointments are among the important available resources. But the importance of the Prime Minister does not derive from the exercise of these prerogatives in isolation. On the contrary, his influence stems from an ability to command the maximum possible amount of information about the political environment and to use this resource in persuading political actors to follow his policy initiatives. Administrative secrecy and collective ministerial responsibility permit the executive to acquire requisite political knowledge without revealing conflicts or divisions which may occur within its ranks. However, the necessity to conceal the process of decision-making at this level in government has sustained the erroneous idea that the executive works in isolation from parliamentary influence and has contributed significantly to the impression that the government acts independently of public opinion.

The Prime Minister's resources will differ from problem to problem and all attempts to enumerate his prerogatives and equate them with his power will flounder. What is required is an accurate understanding of the influences at work on the Prime Minister and how they structure the deployment of his resources. This chapter provides the basis for an assessment of the influence of various actors in the inner circle by outlining its organizational basis, describing the atmosphere of its deliberations, dissecting the policy-making prism and analysing the linkages between the inner circle and Parliament. An accurate conception of the inner circle is required prior to a discussion of Parliament and the roles actors assume in both parts of the legislative system.

THE ORGANIZATIONAL BASIS OF CABINET

The constitutional authority of the Prime Minister and cabinet derives from the fact that the cabinet is a committee of the Queen's Privy Council for Canada and as such tenders advice to Her Majesty's representative, the Governor General. When the crown lost most of its political importance, the cabinet, though not mentioned in the BNA Act, remained the agent of executive authority. As the head of the cabinet, the Prime Minister embodies governmental leadership between and during election campaigns and is the political figure who has the greatest saliency for the public. Members of the governing party accept his preeminent position because their survival as members of Parliament depends to some degree on his personal electoral appeal. His control over ministers, and even deputy ministers, is more complete since both are appointed and dismissed on his personal authority as Prime Minister.

Almost all cabinet ministers are given individual responsibility for administering a department of government or a ministry of state.[5] While policy derives from a multitude of sources, these government departments predominate in providing specific policy initiatives. The development of a welfare state requires a modern bureaucracy which can understand and respond to new demands. Politicians cannot hope to duplicate the expertise which derives from administration, nor the information which comes from permanent contact with groups in the environment. And yet only a minister may carry forward departmental requests to the cabinet or defend departmental policies in the House of Commons. A deputy minister or a senior official may represent his department at cabinet meetings and occasionally speak on a specific point, but he does so only at the request of his minister.[6] Such a relationship between a minister and his department protects departmental officials from public attack and, in theory, concentrates approval or disapproval on the responsible "political" head of the department. As a unit, the ministers act to adopt orders-in-council or to advise the Prime Minister. Such deliberations are private, individual opinions are not publicly voiced, and ministers speak or act only in the name of the entire thirty members of cabinet. Such an arrangement provides cabinet with a protective cloak of secrecy and theoretically allows it to approach each political situation as a collective body.

The increased prominence of cabinet and the Prime Minister in the policy-making process has been accompanied by a conscientious effort to maximize the efficiency of individual members and the cabinet as a whole. The evolution and improvement of the cabinet committee system is the most obvious manifestation of this concern. As late as the Pearson administration, full cabinet was the main vehicle of cabinet decision-making and, though it met somewhat irregularly, it debated and reviewed almost every decision taken in committee. Since Trudeau came to office in 1968, cabinet and committee meetings have been scheduled on a regular basis. More important, committees have practically been given the right to make decisions, not just provide opinions for cabinet consideration. There are now the equivalent of two agendas: one cites items which have been processed by a committee and which require only perfunctory confirmation by cabinet; the other lists subjects on which conflict has been expressed by non-committee members or which the committee has proposed be re-examined in cabinet.

At any one time cabinet is divided into ten to twelve committees. Each committee is chaired by the minister who holds the cabinet portfolio most directly associated with its subject matter. There are five operations committees, each of which handles questions of specific policy content: External Policy and Defence, Economic Policy and Programs, Social Policy, Culture and Information, and Science and Technology. Over the years special committees have been established to solve problems associated with strikes, tax reform, grain sales and security. Planning committees include such illustrious committees as Priorities and Planning and Treasury Board as well as Legislation and House Planning, Federal-Provincial Relations, Government Operations, and the less prominent special council which passes routine orders-in-council. The coordination of the legislative system is primarily the responsibility of Priorities and Planning and Legislation and House Planning, but Treasury Board must be included because of its general supervision of government spending and its responsibility for monitoring new program commitments. Treasury Board and its secretariat prepare economic analyses and expenditure forecasts which are forwarded to the Cabinet Committee on Priorities and Planning for use as general guidelines in the preparation of legislative items. Priorities and Planning, chaired by the Prime Minister and composed of the chairmen of cabinet's standing committees, is concerned with providing an orderly timetable for government activities. Its domination of long-term policy development results from its responsibility to develop goals and priorities for Canada and its status as the Prime Minister's committee. This committee's connection with government departments is parallelled by the concern of Legislation and House Planning with the activities of Parliament. The Leader of the Government in the House of Commons, who is given the title of President of the Privy Council to provide a place for him in cabinet, chairs this committee. From this perspective he can develop a detailed appreciation of the legislative program as it appears in both parts of the legislative system. Together these three committees provide ministers with an opportunity to plan and coordinate the pre-parliamentary stages of the legislative system and to link them to parliamentary activities.

Cabinet and its committees are assembled at least once a week during parliamentary sessions. In the year 1968–69 full cabinet met seventy times and there were three hundred and seventy-eight meetings of its committees. Through the operations of the PCO, the Prime Minister exercises control over the cabinet's agenda although committee chairmen are always consulted about the scheduling of committee items. All items are placed before cabinet in the form of cabinet documents, signed or approved by a minister. The volume of cabinet documents has increased rapidly since World War Two to approximately two thousand in 1972. Even though a document may be directed toward a single committee for decision, it is usually circulated to all cabinet ministers. Each cabinet document is given a number, and a security classification. The desire to uphold cabinet secrecy has infused this process with a measure of ritual where even the use of unauthorized paper or pens has affected submissions to cabinet. Informal communication by telephone and personal conversations about cabinet business add immeasurably to the complexity of cabinet interaction.

All ministers, including the Prime Minister, are expected to bring substantive policy questions before cabinet. As each document comes forward, the responsible minister is required to explain and defend its contents. In practice, each minister is allowed at least one major policy area, some legislative proposals, and the opportunity to place at least one topic on cabinet's list of priority problems. Cabinet cohesiveness, like that of any group, is maintained by encouraging each minister to believe that he will succeed in persuading his colleagues to accept some of his proposals. Even if cabinet conflict emerges over a minister's ideas, they will rarely be totally rejected. Instead, the minister will be provided further opportunities to revise and resubmit his document. While policies are, of course, unequal in their significance for the political system, each minister's ability to initiate and obtain agreement on his legislation affects both his evaluation of his cabinet colleagues and his personal esteem in the inner circle.

The mood of cabinet decision-making is one of informality. Decisions are rarely taken by a systematic rendering of opinion. As in other social contexts, guides or hints are communicated about expected behaviour (a process sometimes referred to as "cue reading") and chairmen manage meetings by advancing through cabinet documents unless dissent is expressed. Prime ministers quickly learn that they intimidate their ministers if they state personal opinions before others have been given a chance to express their ideas. Prime Minister Trudeau usually chairs cabinet by providing each minister the opportunity to develop a personal perspective on each issue and only asserts his authority as chairman to indicate that a cabinet consensus has been attained or a division is apparent. Contemporary cabinet deliberations cannot be compared to a meeting between an all-powerful head of state and his courtiers. They bear closer resemblance to the relationship which might exist between a feudal baron and his independently powerful vassals. In this case the participants are united for the group's interests—especially survival.

The administrative and political support for the Prime Minister and his cabinet has grown immensely since A. D. P. Heeney initiated the development of a cabinet secretariat during the Second World War. This growth in the Prime Minister's Office and the Privy Council Office has contributed both to cabinet's efficiency and to arguments about the covert influence of these bodies in the policy-making process. The PMO is filled through personal appointment by the Prime Minister while the PCO is staffed by permanent public servants. Together they are composed of approximately three hundred personnel. Under the direction of the Principal Secretary the PMO acts as a liaison between the Prime Minister and the bureaucracy via the PCO. It also staffs "political cabinet," which is the organizational expression of cabinet's political and electoral interests. The Clerk of the Privy Council and Secretary to Cabinet (presently Gordon Robertson) directs the PCO which coordinates cabinet activities by setting agendas, taking the minutes of cabinet meetings, and conveying cabinet decisions to the bureaucracy.

Both the PMO and the PCO brief the Prime Minister on issues and alert him to possible ministerial differences. Together they monitor all the information flow within what we shall describe as the policy prism. Plainly these officials do not lack access to the centres of policy-making. The Prime Minister meets two officials from PMO and PCO every day to plan his activities, and other officials from these offices attend all high-level planning sessions, participate in interdepartmental committees and have continual access to ministers during cabinet meetings. They can command prime ministerial and cabinet attention, but they remain essentially amateurs in policy-making. With some notable exceptions, PMO appointees are not specialists in policy areas and the short tenure of PCO officials (except the clerk and deputy secretaries to cabinet) renders them unable to perform the task of policy review carried out in the United States by the Executive Office or in the United Kingdom by the new Central Policy Review Staff.

THE POLICY PRISM

The policy prism is a concept we employ to denote the operations of central institutions in the coordination of government policies and the explication of their legislative details and ramifications for Parliament and the public. Like a light prism, these operations convert undifferentiated phenomena into an organized and recognizable pattern. Within the policy prism the relationships between political goals, governmental activities, budgetary requirements and legislative initiatives are determined. Policies are the culmination of these activities. They provide a long-term governmental perspective in issue areas and structure specific decisions in the legislative system.

In recent years academic students of policy-making have revealed major structural changes in the policy prism. Under Lester Pearson a well-developed system for coordinating departments or formulating priorities within the government did not exist. Pierre Elliott Trudeau installed a more orderly system of decision-making. Cabinet was organized to reflect the essentials of rational policy-making—the efficient pursuit of predetermined goals. In theory, goals would be established and the government would develop policies designed to attain them. Policies would be chosen on the basis of the resources required for their implementation and their relation to other commitments.

Many of these changes were accomplished by adopting for cabinet's use those elements of rational policy-making which had already found expression in the introduction of Program, Planning and Budgeting techniques (PPB) in the public service. This type of budgeting procedure is based on priorities which are set at the cabinet level and communicated to departments via Treasury Board. Departments are obliged to frame their budgetary requirements in terms of goals and objectives. They are also expected to provide a program forecast which will enable cabinet and Treasury Board to improve government planning in subsequent years.[7]

The new structures of rational policy-making have been implemented most thoroughly in the lower levels of the bureaucracy and less completely in the upper echelons. The Cabinet Committee on Priorities and Planning does develop a set of goals which it would like to achieve for Canada. In recent years these general goals have included such vague concepts as social justice, national unity and quality of life. The committee has also developed a list of priority problems such as regional economic expansion, bilingualism, participation, and pollution and has assigned extra resources to their resolution. Such goals and priority areas have been used to prod departments into making new policy proposals and to initiate interdepartmental committees where no clear departmental interest had been established or where more than one department could claim an expertise.

Goals and priorities exert an influence on government spending and on the legislative program. In the budgetary process Priorities and Planning receives information from Treasury Board and the departments about program forecasts. When this information is combined with the fiscal framework from the Department of Finance and cabinet's goals and priorities, the committee is able to develop expenditure guidelines which Treasury Board applies in its assessment of departmental budgetary proposals. By developing these new methods of financial regulation, politicians in the inner circle have strengthened their control over existing programs. The government has also attempted to use goals and priorities in the development of a legislative program. There is the assumption that, given the proper structures, politicians will be able to relate their party's philosophy to the items they intend to introduce in Parliament. The rationalist approach underlying this assumption has not proven as successful in relating goals to items in the legislative system as it has in the budgetary process.[8]

Adherence to a rational model of decision-making necessitates that decision-makers in the inner circle strive for clear and consistent goals. Such clear policy direction has rarely, if ever, been present in Canada. Goals are difficult to establish at any time and recent government experience indicates that they arc usually so nebulous as to be virtually useless. It is politicians who must assume much of the responsibility for the failures of rational policy-making. Without political parties which are devoted to specific legislative programs, a rational model holds only limited promise for actors within the inner circle. No rational technique will help to make choices among goals or to determine how much government expenditure should be devoted to (say) defence as opposed to social welfare measures. In Canada the government has developed organizations and categories based on some aspects of a rational model, but politicians have been unable to adhere to the assumptions inherent in this approach.

The relationship between the legislative program and the government's goals demonstrates some of the difficulties. When the legislative program is being developed, each item is categorized under one of cabinet's goals or priorities. The relationship between the goals, the priorities, and the legislation is broadly intuitive. Ministers do not develop their legislation in response to the government's goals, but use the goals as rhetorical categories to justify their legislation. The relationship between goals and bills is sometimes so tenuous that when legislative proposals arrive at the PCO, officials merely group bills under one of the government's goals or priorities. Many senior politicians, sceptical of the so-called rational structures, do not believe it would be advisable to do otherwise.

The government's inability to achieve all the requirements for rational policy-making has led some academics to suggest that a mixed scanning model more closely approximates actual policy-making behaviour. In such a model, fundamental policies and incremental policies are differentiated by decision-makers. Incremental policy-making is transferred to relatively low levels in the system while the energies of senior policy-makers are concentrated on those policies selected for intense examination. Ideally, all policy areas would eventually be examined and incremental policies could ultimately be related to fundamental ones. But the government's ability to satisfy even the requirements of this model, with its selective application of rational planning, is suspect. In Canada we have created the structures of rational policy-making, but incrementalism predominates within them.

While the central organs of policy-making, buttressed by the techniques of PPB, have attempted to drive governmental goals into the departments, they have faced ministerial and departmental intransigence. There are three fundamental reasons why the Prime Minister has experienced limited success in "top down" policy-making. First, Canadian governments have been unclear about the goals they wished to achieve. Even when the government has attempted to articulate goals, it has discovered that policies cannot be extracted from ringing phrases. Before goals can be used to construct policies, politicians must be agreed on their meaning and their relevance, and they must be accompanied by clear operational goals and adequate program evaluations. Secondly, Canadian governments have often been forced to set aside long-term considerations in the face of short-term contingencies. Rational planning structures could anticipate and manage critical events in an orderly fashion, and the government has given some indication of its willingness to create such structures. Nevertheless, the nature of crises is such that government response cannot always be assessed against existing goals and priorities. Only in the aftermath of the

October crisis of 1970 could the government evaluate its response in the light of its goal of national unity, its priority area of bilingualism, and its myriad of policies involving Quebec. Thirdly, individual ministers must be allowed to develop their own legislative priorities or the mutual trust which cements cabinet will erode. The Prime Minister's need to assure every cabinet member at least limited personal success requires that goals and priority areas be moulded to satisfy departmental and ministerial aspirations. The development of a legislative program based on the need to satisfy stipulated goals is continually plagued by traditional political constraints. New institutional devices are required to develop the legislative program into a coherent and comprehensive instrument for the achievement of government goals.

THE LEGISLATIVE PROGRAM

By tracing the process for producing legislation, the various components of the policy prism can be identified and their contributions assessed. The construction of the legislative program spans activities from the acknowledgement of societal needs through to the assembly of specific legislative items for introduction in Parliament. The successful coordination and scheduling of these activities requires institutions that are sensitive to Canadian values, political realties, and the procedures and demands of the whole legislative system.

The first operation in the development of a legislative program occurs when the Clerk of the Privy Council writes to heads of departments and agencies to request their list of proposed legislation and details about the availability and urgency of each item. This preparatory step normally occurs approximately one year before the parliamentary session for which these items are intended. When they arrive in the PCO, the legislative proposals are classified according to government goals and priorities. The initial analysis of the proposals made by an ad hoc committee of officials from PCO, PMO, the Department of Justice and, more recently, the Office of the President of the Privy Council. Departments which submit proposals may prefer to believe that they are in a constant state of readiness to pursue them, but it is intended that this committee should review departmental proposals in terms of practical impediments such as drafting deadlines, administrative requirements and parliamentary feasibility. Although the committee does not meet again to review this list, its participants advise the leading political actors in the policy prism about the progress of each item in both parts of the legislative system.

The reformulated list of legislative proposals is forwarded to the Prime Minister and the Cabinet Committee on Priorities and Planning. Together they establish the political criteria on the basis of which items are chosen from the list. Either the Cabinet Committee on Legislation and House Planning or an ad hoc committee selects the specific items which will be developed by departments. The process of these cabinet committee meetings is somewhat similar to that suggested by the mixed scanning model in that politicians examine some of the proposals in detail while other proposals receive only a brief mention. Relatively minor bills and departmental housekeeping items are of almost no interest to ministers. On occasion some of these bills have been included on future legislative programs even though literally no one outside the department knew anything about them. The selection process may become so undisciplined that in some circumstances a legislative item could be chosen even though it had a low ministerial or departmental priority. When cabinet finally settles on the content of the program, the PCO employs the decision to prod departments into bringing forward legislation, and the PMO uses it to write the first draft of the Speech from the Throne.

The development of this list of legislative proposals provides, in practical terms, the most important occasion for significant political contribution to the whole program. The list instructs departments and agencies about overall cabinet preferences and in the year prior to an election it also becomes part of the government's total campaign strategy. Since at least a year is required from the construction of this program to the writing of policy memos, the drafting of bills and, finally, the introduction of legislation in Parliament, there is little scope for the addition of items except for emergencies. The constraints of time make it extremely important, therefore, that when the cabinet's decision on the content of the program is circulated to departments, the government's political thrust be at the heart of it. Such emphasis on the government's philosophy is often missing in the face of the demands on the program emanating from items carried over from earlier sessions of Parliament, statutory requirements, departmental aspirations, and recommendations and reports of task forces and royal commissions. As we have pointed out, the presence of a political thrust in the legislative program requires ministers, or the Prime Minister, to have a clear conception of what the government wishes to achieve. If there is no commitment to espoused goals, then ministers will be forced to negotiate, on an individual basis, with groups in the legislative system and may find they are unable to withstand special interests or the conservative forces in the public service.

In addition to the difficulties inherent in relating the legislative program to the government's predetermined goals, the central coordinating agencies have not devised adequate means of forcing individual departments to respond to the legislative program, nor have they succeeded in coordinating the multitude of stages involved in both parts of the legislative system. On occasion, the government has even run out of legislation to place before the House of Commons and at other times there have been so few draft bills available that cabinet has been unable to enjoy the luxury of a selection.

The development of the legislative program imposes a framework and a timetable on departmental formulation of pieces of legislation. The sources of legislation are numerous. Political parties, interest groups, and occasionally members of Parliament suggest legislative initiatives, but it is the administration and evaluation of existing programs which usually provides the inspiration for ministerial and bureaucratic measures.

If a minister merely wishes to make minor administrative amendments to the law, he is likely to submit a legislative proposal which may be channelled quickly through the system. If, on the other hand, he intends to change government policy or emphasis he will be required to follow a more difficult route. He must first submit a policy memorandum to cabinet. The Prime Minister through the PCO will determine which subject-matter committee will receive the memorandum and when it will be placed on their agenda. Prior to the original submission it is likely that interdepartmental committees will have attempted to ensure that the new policy is coherent and consistent with other government activities. It is also their task to anticipate and resolve ministerial conflict which could emerge in cabinet. At the cabinet committee meeting, two perspectives will be brought to bear on the policy memorandum. It will be placed in its widest possible setting and discussed in terms of its political impact. Discussion will also concentrate on the details and technical requirements of the policy. Policies are usually so long in the developmental stages, often being returned to departments for reconsideration, that experienced ministers have been thoroughly briefed by their own officials, been approached by interest groups, and been engaged in lengthy discussions with caucus and individual members of Parliament.

When the complex process of achieving a cabinet decision on the policy memorandum is completed, different governmental structures become involved.[9] Cabinet first approves the legislative proposal for drafting. At this stage the sponsoring department is supposed to provide a comprehensive set of instructions to the drafting office of the Department of Justice so that drafting in both official languages may begin. Usually, however, the original policy memorandum serves as the basis for drafting and because of its general nature draftsmen often encounter inconsistencies and situations in which policy details have not been related to existing Canadian statutes. In the discussion between drafting officials and the sponsoring department, minor policy is made in the resolution of these difficulties. Some officials consider that the final policy impact is influenced almost as much by these details as by the original policy memorandum. "You can have the policy, leave the details to me," has been the philosophy of at least some senior administrators. Moreover, in their quest to provide unity to Canadian law the draftsmen also make what might be called "legal policy inputs." If drafting considerations were made an integral part of policy formation, perhaps some of the practical difficulties could be anticipated and the legal details could be made to serve the general policy intention. In the United

Kingdom preliminary drafts of bills are circulated to all departments to provide extensive opportunities for senior officials to comment on the legal and administrative ramifications.

When the sponsoring minister accepts the draft legislation, it is returned to cabinet via the Committee on Legislation and House Planning. This committee, chaired by the President of the Privy Council, attempts to examine the draft bill clause by clause to ascertain if it accords with the policy memorandum, and to determine the reception it is likely to receive in the House of Commons. In the minority situation following the 1972 election, cabinet ministers used this setting to inform their colleagues of discussions they had held with opposition spokesmen about the passage of their bills. Nevertheless, this committee tends to be preoccupied with the legal expression of government policy. In recent years departments have appended an explanatory memorandum to the draft bill to aid ministers in the discussion of its technical and legal aspects. The chairman is briefed by officials in his own office and by the Legislation and House Planning Secretariat of the Privy Council Office. Draftsmen are always in attendance and lawyers on the committee furnish much of the debate.

If the committee is generally dissatisfied with the draft legislation, it is returned to a subject-matter committee. Normally, however, the committee makes only minor changes, approves the bill, and relays it to cabinet for inclusion on the agenda for items requiring only perfunctory approval. The draft bill is then submitted to the Prime Minister for his signature. The formal transmittal to Parliament occurs when the draft bill, signed by the Prime Minister, is sent to the Clerk of the appropriate House for introduction. At this stage, parliamentary strategy and tactics become paramount and the structures which link the pre-parliamentary and the parliamentary stages of the system go into operation. This does not end cabinet's legislative role either in Parliament or after the successful passage of the bill. Most statutes require the government to develop detailed regulations for the administration of the general provisions and these are given legal authority by orders-in-council, of which cabinet passes approximately six thousand annually.

Coordination of the legislative system has occasionally suffered from inadequate attention to the time required to complete the various stages of the process. On some occasions the government may be without sufficient parliamentary time to handle its available legislation and on others it overtaxes institutions in the pre-parliamentary stages in order to obtain a minimum number of bills. The difficulties may be illustrated by an incident related among members of the Department of Justice. In replying to a command for the immediate production of a very difficult bill, a senior official told the Prime Minister that it reminded him of a story. A young child, after having been promised a baby brother by Christmas, was told by his mother that there was no longer enough time available. Somewhat dejected, he suggested that his mother do what his father would do—"Hire more men!" When cabinet shifts priorities to cope with emergencies or to introduce new ideas, the time difficulties are understandable. But when the government runs out of legislation or demands that Parliament work overtime, it is often due to a lack of coordination in the legislative system which could be corrected by an overhaul of some of the structures.

LINKAGES WITH PARLIAMENT

In a parliamentary form of government it is necessary to remember that the executive and the legislature in combination form the legislative system. In chapter 2 we treated conceptually the links between the executive and the legislature and outlined the functions this system performs. The structures that actually link the institutions in the inner circle with Parliament have often been underestimated in descriptions of the organization of Canadian government. The crucial factor in this linkage is the requirement that members of cabinet hold a position in the House of Commons or the Senate. This simple requirement structures the activities of virtually every institution and the behaviour of every actor in both parts of the legislative system. Neither the legislature nor the executive could operate democratically if ministers did not have to defend in Parliament their legislative proposals and account for the actions of their departments before their parliamentary peers. Bagehot's classic description of cabinet as "a hyphen which joins, a buckle which fastens" may fail to appreciate the contemporary role of the Prime Minister, but it remains the most appropriate metaphor to describe the nature of the executive-parliamentary link.

In addition to the pervasive influence of overlapping membership, several devices exist to bridge activities in both parts of the legislative system. The results of these linkages are reminiscent of open covenants, secretly arrived at. The Throne Speech, which is read by the Governor General in the Senate chambers at the beginning of every session, outlines what has been prepared in the inner circle for presentation to Parliament. It is considered by cabinet to be the most important public statement of its political intentions. It forms the basis for all parliamentary business and as such should be used in evaluating cabinet's performance in governing the country. The Throne Speech consists of a rather vague statement of government goals and the legislative program which the government will place before Parliament. Ideally, the goals and priorities would be the same as those which had been used by the Cabinet Committee on Priorities and Planning to determine departmental priorities and new policy directions. The Throne Speech, which includes a summary of the legislative program discussed earlier, is drafted by the PMO or PCO and, like any important document, is discussed in cabinet. Unfortunately, the utility of this link is diminished by the weakness already present in the relation between goals and legislative proposals.

In 1968 the British practice of attaching a list of all the legislative proposals was included in the Canadian Speech from the Throne. In this fashion the government informed the House of its entire program and thereby encouraged both public servants and parliamentarians to focus on the relationship among the policies and bills. Despite this, and the fact that the cabinet considers it a significant political document, the government was reluctant to have the public judge its accomplishments against the promises in the Throne Speech. In fact, governments often depart from the original list of legislative items and sometimes introduce trial balloon bills merely to ascertain the reactions of

Parliament and the public. In light of this, the government must be prepared to accept that a degree of cynicism will accompany the introduction of any legislation.

Once the Throne Speech has been delivered, the government deposits with Parliament its bills, estimates, regulations, white papers, the reports of royal commissions and advisory committees, and those departmental and agency reports required by statute. The avalanche of documents is accompanied by ministerial answers to thousands of written and oral questions both on the floor of the House of Commons and in its committees. Such activities are organized for the government by the Prime Minister, the Government House Leader and their advisors. Negotiation on substantive issues is required with government followers in the House and on the scheduling of government business with the leaders of other parliamentary parties. Coordination with the government caucus is facilitated by the fact that it always meets the day after Priorities and Planning and the day before full cabinet. The four parliamentary house leaders meet at the beginning of each week to plan the sequence of parliamentary activities.

The task of linking the executive to Parliament falls most heavily on the caucus of the governing party. The government caucus is composed of all party members who support the government. An elected chairman presides over meetings and maintains continuous contact with backbenchers and the House Leader. Cabinet ministers attend caucus and provide information about pending government policy which serves as a foundation for caucus debate. Much of this information is given before caucus committees whose terms of reference parallel, to some extent, cabinet's subject-matter committees and the standing committees of the House of Commons.

This open forum affords opportunities to discuss and reconcile divergent opinions. Backbenchers occasionally use caucus to demonstrate to the Prime Minister that divisions exist in the cabinet, and individual ministers may employ it to illustrate that support exists for their pet projects. Caucus is able to amend, stall and even stop legislation when it is cohesive and has the support of at least some provinces or some interest groups. In recent sessions of Parliament the Liberal caucus has, for example, succeeded in delaying parliamentary consideration of the Young Offenders bill and in halting a minor amendment to the British North America Act which would have increased the size of Parliament. Most of the time, however, the government can obtain, at minimum, acquiescence in its policies and in its schedule of business for the House. The preeminence of the Prime Minister and cabinet exerts unarticulated psychological pressures on caucus members, even within their own jurisdiction. In addition, there are some organizational advantages available to the Prime Minister, particularly his traditional prerogative to review the substance of the entire meeting immediately before adjournment. When Prime Minister Trudeau was openly criticized by an outspoken member of caucus over the government's foreign ownership bill, he utilized this prerogative to reply that all viewpoints had been heard, compromises made and that no new major amendments could be entertained. Frequently, as in this case, outspoken caucus members will encounter opprobrium from their colleagues and feel conscious of the need to refrain from such open confrontations in the future.

Every party in Parliament can claim a direct link with the executive through the consultation among House leaders which takes place each week in the office of the Government House Leader. While each minister conducts a defence of his department in the House, it is the Government House Leader who represents the interests of the entire cabinet in its parliamentary interface. He is in charge of his party's whip and manages the flow of business and the innumerable personal matters which are so important to individual members of Parliament. The House Leader's meeting has become the forum where all parties are told of the manner in which the government intends to use parliamentary resources and the place for negotiation over the scheduling of parliamentary and committee activities. The amount of time devoted to a legislative item and the procedures to be adopted during its passage exert considerable influence on the likelihood of its success. Since Prime Minister Trudeau came to office in 1968, and especially since the 1972 election, the responsibility for negotiating solutions to parliamentary problems has rested heavily on the four House leaders because of their sensitivity to the mood and the sometimes cumbersome mechanisms of the House of Commons.

If we juxtapose the personal influence which the Government House Leader exercises over the parliamentary timetable with the fragmentation of responsibility in the pre-parliamentary part of the legislative system, it can be appreciated that a certain incoherence in policy formation and legislative action may occasionally emerge. It is somewhat incongruous that the government should erect a complex set of institutions for the development of legislation without considering how it might strengthen all the linkages in the legislative system. When the government introduced its monumental tax bill in the fall of 1971, parliamentary advisors soon realized that the bill had been drafted with so few clauses and so many sections that a united opposition could stall the bill by forcing a debate on what sections required a vote, or by debating and voting on almost every sentence. This and other procedural questions required renewed cabinet deliberation and set in motion a series of private meetings between representatives from the Departments of Finance and Revenue, the PCO, the PMO, and the Office of the President of the Privy Council. The issue was finally resolved, with the aid of an all-night parliamentary sitting, but if more foresight and concern for parliamentary procedures had been demonstrated at the drafting stage, some of the obstacles could have been avoided.

There has been a general unwillingness among both parliamentarians and public servants to accept that they share a responsibility for the entire legislative system. The first requirement in the reform of the Canadian legislative system is to improve these inchoate links between the executive and Parliament. If the inner circle is to supply the guns and ammunition for what Trudeau has called Canada's parliamentary "Coney Island shooting gallery" then actors in the inner circle will be obliged to become more aware of the procedures, activities and functions of Parliament.

NOTES

1. The powers and responsibilities of cabinet are discussed in R. M. Dawson and Norman Ward, *The Government of Canada*, 4th ed. (Toronto: University of Toronto Press, 1971); J. R. Mallory, *The Structure of Canadian Government* (Toronto: Macmillan of Canada, 1971); Thomas Hockin, ed., *The Apex of Power* (Scarborough, Ont.: Prentice-Hall, 1971) and G. Bruce Doern and Peter Aucoin, eds., *The Structures of Policy-Making in Canada* (Toronto: Macmillan of Canada, 1971). Detailed comments on cabinet organization and the role of ministers may be found in A. D. P. Heeney, "Mackenzie King and the Cabinet Secretariat," *Canadian Public Administration*, Vol. 10, no. 3 (September 1967), pp. 366-375; Gordon Robertson, "The Changing Role of the Privy Council Office," *Canadian Public Administration*, Vol. IV, no. 1 (Spring 1971), pp. 487-508; Marc Lalonde, "The Changing Role of the Prime Minister's Office," *Canadian Public Administration*, Vol. IV, no. 1 (Spring 1971), pp. 509-537; and Maurice Lamontagne, "The Influence of the Politician," *Canadian Public Administration*, Vol. XI, no. 3, (September 1968), pp. 263-271.
2. See Denis Smith, "President and Parliament: The Transformation of Parliamentary Government in Canada," and F. Schindeler, "The Prime Minister and the Cabinet," in T. Hockin, ed., *Apex of Power*, pp. 22-48.
3. See Walter Stewart, *Shrug: Trudeau in Power* (Toronto: New Press, 1971)
4. Robert Dahl, *Modern Political Analysis*, 2nd ed. (Englewood Cliffs, N.J.: Prentice-Hall, 1970).
5. The leader of the government in the Senate, who is a cabinet member, the President of the Treasury Board and the President of the Privy Council are obvious exceptions.
6. At regular Liberal cabinet office meetings there is the continual attendance of Privy Council officials, the frequent but irregular attendance of the Deputy Minister of Finance and the Secretary to the Treasury Board, and the occasional participation of officials from the PMO and the National Liberal Federation.
7. Detailed discussions of the Treasury Board and the impact of PPB can be found in W. L. White and J. C. Strick, *Policy, Politics and the Treasury Board in Canadian Government* (Don Mills, Ont.: Science Research Associates, 1971); A. W. Johnson, "The Treasury Board and the Machinery of Government in the 1970's," *Canadian Journal of Political Science*, Vol. IV, no. 3 (September 1971), pp. 346-366; and Michael Hicks, "The Treasury Board of Canada and its Clients: Five

Years of Change and Administrative Reform 1966-71," *Canadian Public Administration,* Vol. 16, no. 2 (Summer 1973), pp. 182-205.

8. Some of the limitations of PPB, are discussed in *Planning, Programming and Budgetary Guide* (Ottawa: Queen's Printer, 1968); Economic Council of Canada, *Eighth Annual Review* (Ottawa: Information Canada, 1971).
9. E. A. Driedger, "Legislative Drafting," *Canadian Bar Review,* Vol. 27, no. 3 (March 1949), pp. 291-317.

5. Parliament I: The House of Commons and Senate

In June 1973, two Canadian officers attached to the International Control Commission in Vietnam were believed to be prisoners of the Viet Cong. In the House of Commons, members of Parliament rose to demand assurances of the government, and particularly of the Secretary of State for External Affairs, about the safety of these Canadian representatives. Although the questions received some ministerial response, Mitchell Sharp himself was in Finland attending a conference on European security. It inevitably fell to members of the media to locate Mr. Sharp, elicit his reaction to the kidnapping, and broadcast his views to the Canadian public. In this small drama Parliament had virtually no part nor, indeed, could it have assumed the role played by the media. Parliament does not have the resources to compete with other important structures in society in the mobilization of public opinion. It remains, for purposes of textbook description, the symbol of legitimate authority in the regime, but this event illustrates Parliament's failure to keep pace with other institutions in terms of skills and resources.

The opinions and attitudes Canadians hold about the political system are at least partially determined by the exchange of information and the political discussions between members of the cabinet and representatives of the media. This form of interaction does not encourage the participation of ordinary members of Parliament and inserts into the process individuals who have no constitutional responsibilities. As a result, the centre of political debate has been removed to some extent from the floor of the House of Commons, and the prestige of members and of the institution has suffered. As if to illustrate the difficulties Parliament encounters, a 1964 public opinion survey found that 45 per cent of Canadian respondents believed that Parliament was doing a "poor job" while only 16 per cent felt it was doing a "good job."[1] If this survey even approximates contemporary attitudes, Parliament is experiencing difficulty generating support for itself and is weakened in its ability to perform its multiple functions for society.

While the media have compounded the difficulties Parliament faces in mobilizing public support, they are not the source of Parliament's ineffectiveness. Since the turn of the century the executive has developed policies and legislation largely independent of systematic parliamentary influence, and it has introduced almost all of the legislation that Parliament eventually adopted. The constitution stipulates that it is the government alone which can initiate the expenditure of public monies while Parliament must simply react to executive requests. Cabinet's ability to prevail on legislative and financial matters has been perfected by the existence of cohesive and disciplined parliamentary parties which support cabinet actions in the House of Commons. This development, and the expansion of government activity in the economy, has undermined Parliament's ability to represent political opinion or lead the debate on political issues. The solution does not lie in the return to an age in which Parliament initiated legislation and assumed the tasks of the contemporary executive. What is required is a further and more efficient development of those activities Parliament already performs well and a concentration on those functions which can be performed virtually nowhere else in the legislative system. In this manner Parliament could acquire the status of the primary arena for the debate and the communication of political issues.

THE CONSTITUTIONAL CONTEXT

The major written portion of the Canadian constitution is the British North America Act. While no reference to cabinet is made, the Fathers of Confederation embraced the ruling constitutional principles of the United Kingdom with their emphasis on representation and parliamentary supremacy. The document contains two major sections with direct relevance to Parliament: one on its composition, the other on the extent of its authority.

Part IV of the BNA Act, entitled "Legislative Power," specifies that Canada is to have one Parliament consisting of a Queen, a House of Commons, and an upper house called the Senate. In the bicameral legislature, membership in the lower house is determined through the electoral system. While membership is adjusted occasionally, as dictated by the requirements of electoral law, the House of Commons in 1974 had 264 members elected from individual constituencies in the provinces and territories. The Senate, by contrast, is a totally appointed body whose membership is set at 102 (with provision for the addition of either 4 or 8 members), although it is unusual that the maximum membership is ever attained. On the advice of the Prime Minister, the Governor General appoints senators from five regions in Canada: 24 from the Maritimes, 24 from Quebec, 24 from Ontario, 24 from the western provinces, and 6 from Newfoundland. The obvious provincial inequities are the subject of less controversy than one might expect, first, because of the relatively minor role the Senate has in the legislative system, and second, because the cabinet, not the Senate, has become the main agent in the federal representation of provincial interests.

Provision for the authority of the Canadian Parliament is located in the preamble of the BNA Act which stipulates that Canada is to have a constitution like that of the United Kingdom. The doctrine of parliamentary supremacy was thereby transplanted in Canada, albeit with some adjustments due to the adoption of a federal system and to the fact that Canada could not amend the BNA Act without referral to the British Parliament. Briefly, parliamentary supremacy is a constitutional principle which requires the executive to be responsible at all times to the legislature, while the legislature is neither controlled by the executive nor interfered with by the courts. In both Canada and the United Kingdom the executive is chosen from members of the legislature and must resign if and when the legislature determines that the executive no longer enjoys its support. Constitutionally, the British Parliament may enact legislation on any subject whatsoever. In principle it could even abrogate liberties or abolish the courts. In neither country, however, may the doctrine of parliamentary supremacy be used to restrain a future parliament from exercising its own prerogatives.

In view of executive dominance and the competition of other sectors of society, a constitutional principle like parliamentary supremacy may seem to have little relevance in contemporary political life. Even the BNA Act restricts parliamentary supremacy by specifying those areas of jurisdiction which are the exclusive reserve of the provinces, and demarcating those subjects in the act whose amendment is beyond the authority of Parliament. Nevertheless, this principle still pervades theories about interaction between the executive and the legislature and provides the theoretical foundation for notions such as ministerial responsibility, Parliament's final authority in the collection and appropriation of public monies, and motions of non-confidence in the government.

The British Parliament slowly acquired the rights and privileges now referred to as the supremacy of Parliament. In the initial stages of their development, Parliaments were primarily consultative bodies established at the initiative of barons who had a direct interest in maintaining control of the English king. Although the king did not always act upon the advice proferred, he was required at least to consult his barons. Parliament slowly enhanced its status, first by restricting the king's choice of advisors and then by controlling taxation. Except for brief periods of extreme conflict, relations between the crown and Parliament were mutually beneficial. Parliament forced kings to consult on major policy questions while monarchs like Henry VIII employed Parliament's claim to supremacy to sanction laws unpopular with some sections of the population. Until the British Parliament was reformed in the nineteenth century, it was composed of representatives of traditional elements such as the aristocracy and the church. Because of its composition, Parliament often found itself in sympathy with the crown on contentious issues and many monarchs behaved as if Parliament's role was to help secure their control over the people. Thus, parliamentary supremacy and executive control evolved in tandem as ideas around which the parliamentary process was organized.

By the time Canadians had drafted their major constitutional document, limitations had already been placed on the supremacy of Parliament. Only during the period 1867 to 1906 did the Canadian legislature display the major characteristics of the nineteenth-century British Parliament. By 1913 the procedures which characterize the present relationship between the executive and the legislature in Canada were evolving. The government was beginning to construct a legislative program and to claim for itself the parliamentary time required to realize its objectives.

The principle of parliamentary supremacy allows Parliament to participate in the performance of two major functions, law-making and surveillance. As indicated in chapter 4, those institutions which make the most significant contribution to the initial development of legislation are in the inner circle. Nevertheless, Parliament is quite correctly viewed as that part of the legislative system which transforms bills into statutes by moving them through various stages during which they are exposed to the public, subject to partisan attack, and refined into acts of Parliament. Much parliamentary timc is also consumed in the scrutinizing of government expenditure, the oversight of administration, and the interpellation of cabinet ministers. This surveillance function results in some of the most publicized parliamentary activities.

In passing laws and in supervising executive actions, Parliament acquires the ability to perform other functions for the legislative system. The fact that all functions have intangible aspects and are interrelated makes it extremely difficult to distinguish among them or to measure their performance, as we shall see in Chapter 8. In the case of legitimation, Parliament may be said to perform this function in a manifest way when it votes on and approves legislation. It performs the same function in a latent manner simply by holding regular meetings and debating government actions. When Parliament meets in an emergency sitting to discuss a crisis situation, law-making may be the operation carried out, but often a conflict management function is performed as a consequence. In the following section we will describe how both the House of Commons and the Senate participate in the making of laws and in the surveillance of the executive. In each case it is important to understand that these operations may contribute to, or detract from, the performance of other functions.

THE LEGISLATIVE PROCESS IN THE HOUSE OF COMMONS

To most outsiders and to some participants, Parliament consists of a mystery of relics, dignitaries, and ceremonial debates. Many of the rituals originated in Britain with the struggle between Parliament and the crown, and while their practical significance may be obscure, they are important symbolic outputs of the legislative system. The procedures of Parliament have also been influenced by our British heritage.[2] The most important rules for the conduct of parliamentary business in Canada are entitled "standing orders." These rules should be viewed both as a series of impartial routines designed to facilitate the debate and transaction of parliamentary business, and as a political weapon which aids the executive in governing the country. When ministers answer questions during question period the rules are intended primarily to permit the open criticism of government activities. On the other hand, the restrictions placed on the use of parliamentary time by private members illustrate how the rules have been progressively manipulated since 1913 to allow the government to manoeuvre its legislative program through Parliament. Despite the tensions that exist between the two objectives of parliamentary rules, participants have normally achieved a consensus on procedure which has helped to maintain the viability of the institution. Only in 1968 did this consensus break down to the extent that the government had to use closure to terminate debate on new procedures.

The control and the allocation of available parliamentary time is determined generally by constitutional requirements and specifically by procedural rules. Parliaments are summoned and dissolved by the Governor General on the advice of the Prime Minister. Since there is no fixed date for elections, their occurrence is, in practical terms, determined when the Prime Minister, for whatever reason, chooses to dissolve Parliament or when he clearly loses the confidence of the House of Commons. Constitutionally, an election must be held at least once every five years and it is these events which effectively mark the commencement and the termination of parliaments. Regardless of their length, parliaments must meet in at least one session every year. The beginning of each session is marked by a Speech from the Throne and the termination by the ceremony of prorogation. Following World War Two, sessions normally began in the fall and ended in the spring. Recently, partially due to the prevalence of minority governments, the scheduling of sessions has been less consistent and planning has been made more difficult. Members of the House of Commons have often been required to sit for more days during the year, and the traditional summer recess has been placed in jeopardy.

The standing orders state the daily time dimensions within which Parliament has chosen to operate. Except for rare emergency sittings, Parliament sits every weekday, and each sitting follows a normal pattern. After opening ceremonies, time is set aside for formal proposals which, in parliamentary language, are known as motions. Members of the government use this opportunity to lay official documents before the House and to announce government policy to Parliament. Both the government and private members employ this period to make motions about the business of the House of Commons and its committees. The Parliamentary Secretary of the President of the Privy Council may then read ministerial answers to written questions placed on the order paper by members of the House. The forty-minute oral question period follows. It is the best attended event in the parliamentary day and at least one prime minister, John Diefenbaker, has regarded it as the most important. Orders of the day, a period during which government business or opposition resolutions are considered, occupies the attention of the House until 5:00 p.m. It is attended by at least one minister and by scattered representatives from each of the parties. Before dinner, time is set aside for the bills and the resolutions of private members. When the House meets in the evening it is usually between 8:00 p.m. and 10 p.m. to consider government business. On three days of the week this is followed immediately by a debate on the motion to adjourn. This thirty-minute debate, known to parliamentarians as the "late show," consists of three short debating periods monopolized by backbenchers and parliamentary secretaries.

The time allotted to some activities is specified in the standing orders, while the time assigned to others requires negotiation among the parties. In general, the rules limit speeches to forty minutes. While members must rise in their place and be recognized, the choice of speakers is determined by a list of members drawn up by the party whips. The traditional right of privy councillors to be recognized before others is usually respected by the Speaker. When the rules do not specify the scheduling of events in the House negotiations between the House leaders, and occasionally the whips, are used to resolve disputes. Even in these meetings procedural norms exert an effect. In the unusual event that the House leaders are unable to agree on time allocation, closure or filibuster of debate may occur.

a. *Law-making*

In Chapter 4 the creation of a legislative program and the development of a single legislative item in the pre-parliamentary stages were treated in some detail. It was clear from that description that the pre-parliamentary stages are used to develop policy proposals and draft legislation, but that formal law-making only begins when the draft legislation is introduced in Parliament in the form of a bill. Neither committees of the House nor the House itself actually legislates; this practice died in Britain in the first half of the nineteenth century and at the turn of the twentieth century in Canada. The government is the main initiator of legislation and pilots the bills through the House and committees on the strength of its majority. A bill, when it is passed by Parliament, is called an act, and only after royal assent and proclamation does it become a law.

The passage of bills through Parliament bears some similarity to their movement in the inner circle: debate is often protracted, progress sporadic, and precise scheduling difficult. At each of the pre-parliamentary stages, policy proposals were infused with new qualities—priority labels, detailed amendments, and legal form. To some degree parliamentary consideration represents a continuation of this process, but two new dimensions are added. Parliamentary examination is more formal and more open. Formal action and consent is required at virtually every parliamentary proceeding, and while this sphere of law-making is more public than any other, paradoxically, the ritual occasionally serves to conceal the process more effectively than ministerial oaths of secrecy.

In the pre-parliamentary stages, legislative items are differentiated primarily on the basis of availability, urgency and compatibility with political goals. Parliament distinguishes among bills on constitutional and legal grounds in two major ways. First, legislation may be divided into private and public bills. Private bills apply to specific individuals or groups of people and are usually designed to accomplish a particular and narrow purpose. They are required to incorporate insurance firms, for example, or, until recently, to grant divorces for the provinces of Quebec and Newfoundland. Public bills are of two types: those which are sponsored by the cabinet and consume the bulk of parliamentary time, and private members' bills which are sponsored by individual members of Parliament and are rarely permitted to become law. Public bills may also be redivided into financial and non-financial varieties. Those requiring expenditure are known as money bills and are always introduced by the government. Since different types of bills must meet different requirements in Parliament, actors in both parts of the legislative system must observe these distinctions.

The movement of legislation through Parliament may be divided into seven formal stages. At each step, timing decisions contribute significantly to the eventual success or failure of legislative proposals. After receiving final cabinet approval, the draft legislation is initialled by the Prime Minister and deposited with the Clerk of the appropriate House. The initial motion is for leave to introduce the bill in the House and at a subsequent sitting a first reading motion is introduced, usually by the sponsoring minister. Its acceptance, which is normally a matter of course, allows the bill to be printed and given a number (a "C" prefix if it originates in the Commons, an "S" prefix if it originates in the Senate). If the bill is a money bill the Parliamentary Council drafts a document called a royal recommendation which states, either generally or specifically, the purposes for which money is being appropriated. It is subsequently used as a frame of reference to determine the validity of proposed amendments. The bill is now on the order paper, which is the schedule of pending parliamentary business. It has been brought to Parliament's attention and, if it is a government bill, it can be called by the Government House Leader to form the basis for debate during the period set aside for government business.

The next stage of the process is the second of three readings. Out of courtesy and political considerations, the government announces the general schedule of parliamentary business one week in advance, but no notification is required once the bill is in the House. During second reading the Speaker enforces strict rules of relevancy and permits no amendments, because this stage is designed to focus attention on the principles of the bill. Sponsoring ministers almost always appear to defend their bill and the government and opposition front benches monopolize debate. This stage usually takes one or two days though there is no requirement that they be consecutive. When debate is completed, standing orders 74(1) and 74(2) stipulate that "unless otherwise ordered" a bill must be sent directly to a standing, special, or joint (Senate and House) committee where the detailed consideration of bills is commenced. Committee of the Whole House, which is the House sitting as a committee with rules relaxed and the Deputy Speaker presiding, has lost its significance except for the detailed examination of bills designed to raise revenue. A major example was the discussion of the 1972 tax bill in Committee of the Whole. This procedure allows all members a chance to speak on the bill and the government an opportunity to control events more closely than it can in standing committees.

Clause-by-clause consideration of bills is almost always the task of the committee system. In this third stage of legislation, the several standing committees are able to meet and consider bills simultaneously. Debates may take place and amendments be moved on every clause of the bill. While most amendments originate in the opposition, the government itself may take this opportunity to amend the legislation. As far as committee members are concerned, the overriding difficulty is to decide what committees are supposed to do with bills. Some members believe that committees should be concerned only with the technical questions such as shaping the details of bills, making refinements and preventing administrative oversights. But others believe that the examination of bills by committees should provide an opportunity to investigate the general policy behind the bill. One study of the present committee system found that there were thirty-five amendments to the Radio Act (Bill C-163), many of which came from the opposition, and a large number of these amendments were accepted by the government.[3] Most of the amendments were in the "refining the bill" category and therefore should be considered technical. On occasion, however, there have been changes in the substance of bills. In the 28th Parliament the language bill and breathalyzer legislation both had amendments put by backbenchers which were accepted by the government. In the minority situation of the 29th Parliament more amendments were directed to the essentials of the bills. Major changes in legislation took place, for example, on the election expenses and the wiretapping bills. However, the government is not always responsive to backbench initiative. In 1971 the opposition conducted a filibuster in committee on the Farm Marketing Products Act before the government made any changes. On amendments to money bills the powers of committees are severely limited by the rule that the object, scope, and purposes of a royal recommendation or the terms on which money is granted, cannot be changed by a private member. Unless a proposed new expenditure can be interpreted as consistent with the royal recommendation it is constitutionally invalid. Not even a minister is permitted to make amendments: he must withdraw the bill and introduce a new royal recommendation. The only remedy open to the private member and the committee is to either reduce or vote against the amount of money recommended. Distinguishing between valid and invalid amendments can be an exceedingly difficult task. In order to determine whether a proposed amendment violates the royal recommendation a test is used by the Chair and by the advisors who counsel committee chairmen. It involves asking two questions: first, could the proposed amendment be reasonably expected to require the spending of monies, and second, if so, is the spending of that amount of money for that specific purpose authorized in the royal recommendation? Only if the second question can be answered positively is the amendment proper. Due to the fact that a royal recommendation hovers between being as precise as a statute and merely a statement of intent, there is always considerable room for difference of opinion in borderline cases. While it is obvious that a major increase is beyond the scope of the royal recommendation, an amendment to the Small Business Loans Act which sought to add the Alberta Treasury Board to the list of lending agencies was not an obvious violation. However, like almost all of these backbench initiatives, it was ruled out of order.

The fourth step of the parliamentary process is the report stage, so called because it refers to the reporting of the amended bill back to the House. Debate ranges over both the principles and the details of the bill. Amendments defeated in committees may be reintroduced in the House, a practice which consumes valuable time and tends to negate the objective of committee consideration. Nevertheless, opposition members may use this opportunity to publicly advocate their proposals while the government uses report stage to "correct" committee amendments or to launch new ones.

By comparison with the first four stages of parliamentary consideration, the final proceedings may seem somewhat perfunctory. At least twenty four hours must elapse before the fifth stage, third reading, can be embarked upon, although the House may waive this time restriction by unanimous agreement. Debate during third reading is not impossible or unknown, but it must be commenced at the opposition's insistence.

The sixth stage in the process covers Senate consideration (unless the bill was introduced in the Senate) which is often brief and normally attracts little public attention. Procedures resemble those of the House of Commons and most of the refining of legislation is confined to the committee system. When the Senate does react it is frequently to challenge provisions considered harmful to business. The Banking, Trade and Commerce committee is by far the most active standing committee. Its members propose most of the legislative amendments and, on the strength of their business contacts, some senators can influence a bill's consideration in the House of Commons.[4] On rare occasions the Senate may obstruct the work of the House. In December 1973, the Senate amended the wire-tapping bill, C-176. This action deleted a clause which had been opposed by the minority Liberal government but sponsored by a majority of the members of the House of Commons. Such action would not be tolerated if it occurred repeatedly. In this particular case the House repassed the bill with the amendment intact and the Senate capitulated.

In the final stage of legislation, the executive, in the garb of the Governor General, returns to seal the process by royal assent which is given in the Senate, usually to several bills at once. This does not mean that the bill is automatically law on that day. With greater frequency in recent years, statutes require proclamation, a decision usually entrusted to the departments involved but requiring the approval of cabinet through a special committee of Council.

The entire legislation process is so complex that it can easily become unworkable. Particular parties and groups in Parliament are continuously given opportunities to thwart the conversion of bills into statutes and the government is often forced to abandon projects because of a time shortage. In the final hours of the fourth session of the 28th Parliament the government requested unanimous consent to proceed immediately with third reading of the Family Income Security bill. One member denied permission and this single action stopped proceedings on the legislation. Since FISP was never reintroduced this action effectively killed the bill. Many bills in the government's program are left on the order paper and must be reintroduced in the next session, regardless of their previous progress. In the parliamentary theatre many performances occur simultaneously and efficient government direction is required to ensure that its priority items survive without endless compromise. In a majority government situation, the opposition may be unable to prevent the passage of a single bill, but, despite its advantages, the government rarely succeeds in achieving its whole legislative program.

b. *Surveillance*

In accordance with the constitutional principle of parliamentary supremacy, the Canadian Parliament engages in another set of activities that can be described generally as surveillance of the executive. Between elections the legislature must find techniques to hold the executive responsible and such surveillance can take many forms. In fact, if the term is defined very generally, almost every parliamentary activity, including legislative amendment, could be considered an aspect of surveillance. In this book the concept will refer more specifically to the means by which Parliament demands information and justification from the executive for the general direction of policy and for the detailed activities of government, expressed, for example, in the estimates and subordinate legislation. An adversary style of question and debate often accompanies the performance of the surveillance function.

The opportunity for parliamentary scrutiny of specific government policy is best afforded by a consideration of departmental estimates. The estimates represent the government's projected spending patterns for the year and they are prepared by the Treasury Board Secretariat for the forthcoming fiscal year, April 1 to March 31. The final document is the "Blue Book" which contains the estimates. When the estimates are ready to be tabled, a message is obtained from the Governor General pursuant to section 54 of the BNA Act. Parliament must formally extend or withhold its approval of the estimates. Parliament is, therefore, the final arbiter of government appropriations in Canada even though it is the executive which actually does the spending. The government is prohibited from spending money for purposes which have not been specifically approved by Parliament.

Before the final estimates reach the parliamentary stage, their precise composition has been the subject of extensive deliberation among departmental officials and budgeting and cost accounting experts. The introduction of PPB and the strengthening of budgetary control in the hands of the Treasury Board Secretariat and the Treasury Board itself has enhanced the process of centralized control over expenditure in the departments. With the possible exception of the post-audit process,[5] which is the responsibility of the Auditor General who reports directly to the House of Commons, Parliament has nothing to compare with the techniques of control the government imposes upon itself. Parliament has barely managed to remain stationary in the evolution of appropriations control, and by comparison with the executive it has experienced a relative decline.

Prior to the procedural reforms introduced in 1969, the main government estimates were considered in Committee of Supply which was actually the House meeting under another name with the rules relaxed and the Speaker replaced in the Chair by another member.[6] The motion to enter Committee of Supply gave members an opportunity to launch into a wide-ranging debate not necessarily on financial matters. In 1913, 1955 and 1965 time restrictions were placed on the business of Supply and in 1969 the whole procedure was replaced by the referral of main estimates to the Commons standing committees. The main estimates are usually referred to Parliament during the final week of February and to committees of the House on or before March 1. This is accomplished by the passage of a government motion on which there can be neither debate nor amendment. Once the main estimates are referred, the standing committees are required to report them back not later than May 31.[7] If they have not been reported by that date, Standing Order 58 (14) provides that they "shall be deemed to have been reported." Thus, there is no requirement that the committees formally approve the estimates.

The new procedure which refers estimates to standing committees has not been accompanied by a new way of approaching them. The order of reference is at least partially responsible for this state of affairs. It is so wide that it implies that every item in the Blue Book should be considered while not commanding an in-depth investigation of any department. Members of Parliament devote their committee time primarily to general inquiries about the policies and administrative practices of the department whose estimates are being considered. This tendency has been enhanced by the committee's ability to summon and question officials. In the old Committee of Supply departmental officials occupied seats in the aisle of the floor of the House of Commons, advised their ministers on questions, and escaped direct interrogation. During the second session of the 28th Parliament there were a total of 134 meetings of the standing committees on estimates and these were attended by 352 officials. With officials available in the new system the consideration of estimates has become primarily a device for gathering information.

Committees meet irregularly and their members pose few questions which concern the cost of government programs, rarely admonish ministers, and even less frequently reduce specific expenditure items. Few chairmen of standing committees consider this an opportunity to question the government on matters relating directly to cost. This lack of cost consciousness is neither a new nor a uniquely Canadian phenomenon. As early as 1902 the Committee of Supply in the United Kingdom was regarded as a political forum and the opinion developed that simply controlling costs was of little purpose unless it was also possible to examine the policies and administration of government departments.

While Canadian committees provide a forum where members may be educated by the bureaucracy in the operations of particular departments, they lack a permanent staff and there is an absence of the specialization necessary to launch detailed investigations. Estimates reports in Canada are exceptionally brief and, since the government is not required to take action, both the government and the House generally ignore appended recommendations. Some committees persist in the belief that every estimate should be considered and voted on separately as in the old Committee of Supply and, in deference to this notion, considerable committee time is devoted to the formal passage of votes. It was expected that the introduction of PPB, with a budget format based on objectives, would provide Parliament with a new opportunity to offer a more fundamental critique of government spending.[8] Although it is somewhat early to assess properly the impact of PPB, the fact that MPs operate without the program information on which the government bases much of its planning suggests that Parliament is not making full use of the new budget procedures. Members are still mainly concerned with programs that have been added or eliminated, not with the strategic aspects of control which PPB is designed to emphasize. Specific expenditures, particularly if they relate to constituency problems, remain the focus of members' interests. Moreover, the fact that no committee considers the totality of departmental estimates means that no institution is made responsible for a comparative study of the expenditure patterns of all departments. It should be possible for Parliament to compare the estimates of one department with those of another, and to improve its capacity to analyse the operations of on-going government programs when requests are made for refunding. The United Kingdom Expenditure Committee carries out precisely this type of investigation. In short, all of these considerations indicate that Parliament lacks the institutional resources, and members the desire to exercise a proper surveillance of government spending.

It has long been accepted that for practical reasons Parliament must delegate much of its legislative authority to the executive.[9] Parliament does not have the time to debate the detailed rules that must be used to implement policy, nor does it have the technical expertise. Thus, in many cases, Parliament provides only a framework for the rule-making that will take place in the bureaucracy. Until recently, the Canadian Parliament has expressed little interest in examining how this delegated authority is exercised. For many years Canada lagged behind other parliamentary systems in providing for the publication of rules and regulations and their tabling in Parliament.[10] The Regulations Act of 1950 imposed these requirements on most subordinate legislation (most regulations are now published in the Canada Gazette), but Parliament still lacked opportunities to systematically review the exercise of delegated legislation. In Britain, by contrast, some pieces of legislation stipulate that Parliament must pass a resolution affirming the exercise of delegated authority and others provide for the annulment of rules and regulations. Few Canadian laws contain such requirements. The Canadian Parliament has permitted the extensive delegation and re-delegation of its authority and has agreed to bills with sweeping enabling clauses that provide a great scope for the formulation of regulations. But it has not developed special techniques to review delegated legislation and relies instead on other surveillance devices.

In 1969 the House of Commons Special Committee on Statutory Instruments made several recommendations to improve the surveillance of delegated legislation.[11] The committee was concerned with imprecision in the formulation of regulations, the lack of public debate and consultation, and the inadequacy of parliamentary control. The Statutory Instruments Act, 1971 incorporates many of the committee's recommendations including the establishment of a parliamentary committee, much like the Scrutiny Committee in the United Kingdom, to which most statutory instruments will automatically be referred. It is intended that this committee report to Parliament on what it considers to be the unusual or unwarranted use of delegated powers. However, reports must reflect on the application of policy, not on its merits. To be effective, therefore, this committee will require an absence of partisanship, expertise among its members and, particularly, a legal and administrative staff.

Although the committee's membership has been decided (it is a joint Senate-Commons committee), the government has been noticeably slow in activating it. It is not surprising that the government shows restrained enthusiasm for this type of body. However, if minority governments continue, the question of delegation may become more important. Support for a minority government is almost always tentative and in this situation opposition parties may be more inclined to insist on a review of decisions. In January 1974 the government introduced the Energy Supplies Emergency Act, Bill C-236, which permitted government action to preserve petroleum supplies during a national emergency. The parties subsequently agreed to an amendment which provides Parliament with an opportunity to debate and possibly revoke the government's action. In the same month the opposition parties limited the government's authority to change the conditions under which an export tax on crude oil could be imposed (Bill C-245). In both of these cases Parliament insisted on its role in supervising delegated legislation.

Oral question period is the most celebrated forum for continuous, open criticism of government policy. As a surveillance device it has the attractive feature of being an uninterrupted forty-minute period which the executive cannot avoid. Question period is unconnected to the routine processing of legislation and it stands out as a time when the opposition assumes its most militant posture. To strengthen the inquisitorial nature of the proceeding, cabinet ministers seldom receive advance notice of the content of questions. The types of questions and their order are an important part of the tactics of parliamentary leadership. In the Conservative party, for example, questions are usually selected at a daily meeting in the opposition lobby attended by the Leader, the House Leader, the chairman of caucus and members with particular interests. Questions are selected for their potential political benefit and discussion often centres on the opening question of the day, the symbolic core of opposition grievance.

In addition to the structural qualities which make the oral question period a potent weapon, it is also the event which daily attracts the greatest attention from observers of the Canadian Parliament. The constant badinage during question period provides political journalists with a continuous source of material. In addition, it brings party leaders together and thus holds the promise of newsworthy surprises. Largely in response to the attention of the media, and partly because of possibilities for direct participation, members of Parliament also turn out for question period in greater numbers and with greater regularity than for any other occurrence in the parliamentary day.

Even with these inherent advantages, question period has become an object of criticism. It is clear, for example, that it is no longer of sufficient length to accommodate all of the questions members wish to raise, and opposition members object to questions emanating from the government backbenches. Cabinet ministers criticize what they maintain are purely partisan questions, backbenchers claim that cabinet denigrates question period by refusing to supply direct answers, and academics profess that too many oral questions are trivial, information-gathering devices. Moreover, academics and backbenchers combine in their criticisms of the present restrictive disclosure policy and the procedural rules which permit ministers to refuse to answer a question without providing a justification.

These criticisms stem from a belief that question period can be improved from a procedural point of view and while this position is undoubtedly valid, a more fundamental weakness exists. Most parliamentarians seem unable to structure debate in question period around competing party policies or philosophies. Many of the questions are orchestrated for the sole purpose of embarrassing the government. Implicit alternatives are infrequent companions of most questions. Thus, questions appear desultory and, apart from the facts around which questions are organized, there is little to link one question to another or one question period to the next. Effective parliamentary surveillance requires new procedures for question period and the existence in Parliament of a few fundamental ideas about governing which clearly distinguish one party or faction from another.

In their search for new modes of surveillance members of Parliament sometimes succeed in detracting from the major opportunities that already exist. During the period referred to earlier in this chapter as motions, private members, primarily from the opposition, often attempt to obtain unanimous consent to present a motion without notice for a "pressing and urgent necessity." Ostensibly Standing Order 43 provides an opportunity for postponing regular business for an emergency debate. Unfortunately, members often use "43s" simply to raise controversial questions in the knowledge that they will attract the attention of the media and they are unlikely to receive the unanimous consent required to proceed with debate. The abuse of this rule restricts the time Parliament has at its disposal and, because they directly precede the oral question period, such motions detract attention from the main questions of the day.

A major proportion of the House time devoted to surveillance is consumed by the Budget and Throne Speech debates and by what are referred to as "opposition days." Parliamentarians are permitted eight days to debate the Address in Reply to the Speech from the Throne. This procedure provides Parliament with a relatively lengthy period for the criticism of only vaguely worded policy announcements. The lack of depth in the policy debate is implicitly acknowledged by the relaxation of rules regarding relevancy—a tradition which encourages backbench speeches on local issues. The Budget Debate consists of six days of discussion on the government's taxation proposals and general financial policy. The debate, which follows the speech by the Minister of Finance, is similar to the Throne Speech debate in that rules of relevancy are not strictly enforced. Unlike the Throne Speech, however, the days set aside for debate are not required to be consecutive and this prevents a prolonged hiatus in the passing of legislation. On the other hand, this procedure wastes parliamentary time because those debates which do not take place directly after the Budget Speech receive almost no attention from the press or the public.

The opposition parties now have at their disposal a definite amount of parliamentary time to be used for the purpose of general surveillance and criticism. When the Committee of Supply was erased from the parliamentary timetable in 1969 the opposition parties were accorded a total of twenty-five days (plus three days for supplementary estimates) divided unequally among three supply periods during which opposition motions could be debated.[12] These "opposition days" were designed to compensate for the lack of debate on supply under the new rules and it was originally assumed that motions would refer to financial matters. In practice the parties merely divide the opposition days among themselves and use the opportunity to force debates on topical motions which deplore the government's behaviour or urge a particular course of action. Committee reports on estimates have rarely been used as a foundation for debate. For example, in the second session of the 28th Parliament only one of the twenty-four supply motions presented by the opposition parties mentioned the estimates.

The government retains the ultimate responsibility for deciding the precise days to be allotted for opposition motions. Unlike the procedure in question period, twenty-four-hour notice must be given of the content of the opposition resolution. This period provides government officials with an adequate opportunity to prepare detailed briefs on which ministers may base their replies. In these debates, as in the Budget and the Throne Speech debates, the opposition is handicapped by its lack of technical knowledge. The government is buttressed, not only by its public service, but also by interest groups which continuously attempt to inform the government of all the technical requirements of policy.

Frequently, the opposition does not even use all of the days it has at its disposal. In the performance of the surveillance function, the opposition commands a large proportion of parliamentary time. However, when the outcome of votes in the House of Commons is determined in advance by party loyalties, and discussion takes place in the shadow of expert opinion, the purpose of parliamentary debate is questionable. It should be understood that Canadian parliamentarians only very rarely aspire to change the opinions of uncommitted members in the chamber. When debate is not simply for the record, it is designed to appeal beyond individual party loyalties to the sensitivities of the government, the civil service and public opinion. Only if this transmittal can be accomplished will Parliament succeed in holding the executive responsible for its actions in such a manner as to generate support for Parliament, the government and for the individuals who occupy roles within the regime. Debate between honourable members is not necessarily communication with other institutions or individuals. Research has shown that debates rarely affect the actions of public servants or the public. Communication requires that debates have immediate and recognizable meaning and be transmitted directly and without interference. Parliamentary surveillance should not be viewed as a series of debates among members as much as a "thinking out loud process" about the nation's major issues. For this type of debate to be effective, Parliament needs to find new ways of informing public opinion, including the employment of the most recent communications technology. Television is the most attractive initial step toward a resolution of communication problems, but a prerequisite to its introduction will be the removal of some of the mystery of parliamentary procedure.

THE SPECIAL ROLE OF THE SENATE IN THE LEGISLATIVE SYSTEM

Few changes have been made in the Senate's composition or its activities since the Fathers of Confederation made provision for it in the British North America Act. Apart from a 1965 amendment to the act, which requires senators to resign at the age of 75, the Senate persists in much the same form as the Fathers envisaged. Although the colonies had experimented with elected and appointed upper houses and dissatisfaction had been expressed with both, there was a consensus on the necessity for an upper house in the new federation. The provision of an assembly of unelected senators would effectively balance the principle of popular representation which governed the composition of the lower house. The Fathers of Confederation harboured a deep suspicion of the virtues of unqualified democracy and were anxious to establish what George-Etienne Cartier called "a power of resistance to oppose the democratic element."[13] The Senate would also be used to represent property. Contrary to the British tradition, there would be no hereditary titles and senators would not represent a special class in society, but a prospective senator would be obliged to own property valued at $4,000 in the province represented. The Senate's composition was also designed to allay concern that the provinces would lack direct representation in the new Parliament. The powers of the central government appeared awesome, but when the provinces were guaranteed representation in an assembly whose announced purpose was to exert a conservative, protective influence, Confederation became a more palatable prospect.

Agreement on the composition of the Senate was instrumental in securing Confederation, but there was no explicit agreement on the specific role the Senate was to exercise in the legislative system. It was clear that there was to be no equality between the two chambers and that the cabinet should be responsible to the Commons and not the upper house. According to John A. Macdonald, the second assembly would "never set itself in opposition against the deliberate and understood wishes of the people."[14] Yet the Senate was not denied a role in the legislative process. No constraints were placed on the Senate's formal authority because, as Macdonald declared, the Senate "would be of no value whatever were it a mere chamber for registering the decrees of the Lower House."[15] A balance of powers was intended, but a dilemma has emerged. "If it [the Senate] rejects or drastically amends a bill for social or moral reform, it is condemned by impatient reformers as reactionary, autocratic and perhaps immoral. If it is quiescent, it is assumed to be a fifth wheel on the government coach."[16]

The Senate has been restrained in its law-making and surveillance activities. The Senate amendment of government legislation has declined to about 10 per cent of the bills introduced and normally the House of Commons agrees to the amended version. The tendency of the Senate to amend government bills increases appreciably when the majority of senators do not belong to the government's party in the House of Commons. The actual rejection of important government legislation is very unusual (although amendment may be tantamount to rejection as it was in 1961 on the government's customs tariff legislation). Money bills cannot even be introduced in the Senate and there has been a continual dispute between House and Senate officials over the latter's right to amend money bills. The Senate has amended such bills but in practice it has never exercised any formal financial control. In all these facets of law-making the Senate is subordinate to the House of Commons. This is primarily because the unelected senators have weak lines of communication with the political environment and are isolated from the pre-parliamentary structures of the legislative system.

However, the Senate could be considered an active legislative refinery. Senators have demonstrated assiduity in the consideration of certain types of legislation, and when unanticipated changes are required in government bills the Senate is a convenient place to make amendments. Particularly in the area of private bills the Senate has departed from its relatively passive law-making role. Private bills, as discussed earlier, are extremely limited in their scope. They apply to individuals, corporate "persons," or charitable organizations, many of which require legislation to obtain authority or avoid responsibility. Before 1968 the bulk of this legislation consisted of divorce bills from Quebec and Newfoundland whose provincial courts, up until that time, were not empowered to hear divorce cases. Most private bills are introduced in the Senate where the fee is lower and where enough time exists to guarantee thorough treatment. Procedure on private bills is designed to protect the rights of third parties. For example, interested persons must be informed of the bills' intentions by publication and neither House will examine private bills in Committee of the Whole.

It is difficult for the Senate to participate actively in the performance of a surveillance function because the executive has never considered itself responsible to the upper house. Cabinet ministers, with the exception of the Government Leader in the Senate, are rarely drawn from Senate ranks, since the House of Commons demands the opportunity to confront the entire executive. Nevertheless, the Senate has established itself as an investigative body capable of undertaking the type of study associated with royal commissions. The Senate committees on the media and on poverty in Canada are examples of the capacity of senators to bring their experience and skills to bear on contemporary problems. It would seem reasonable to propose that the Senate ought to expand its surveillance role as a watchdog of the federal bureaucracy. A joint Senate-Commons committee on delegated legislation was finally established during the 29th Parliament. The sharing of responsibility in this neglected area should provide a more comprehensive survey of delegated legislation. It should be possible for members of both the Commons and Senate to participate in the performance of this surveillance function without conflict, and indeed cooperation may become a necessity if the pressure on the time available to parliamentarians continues to increase.

The fact that the Senate has occasionally clashed with the popularly elected lower House in the areas of law-making and surveillance does not make it an anomalous, outmoded institution. In a federal system an upper House, with representatives from the various sections of the nation, is often considered a necessary institutional device for representation and integration. In a multicultural and bilingual country it can also be argued that national viability is enhanced if the upper House can aid in the performance of a legitimation function. It is the centre of parliamentary ritual, where the Speech from the Throne is read and royal assent accorded. Despite these possibilities the image of the Senate is such that none of the functions of integration, representation and legitimation are performed with particular success. The obvious loyalty and regard shown by Canadians toward the crown, and the sarcastic barbs that are aimed at the Senate constitute a strange anomaly in the Canadian political system. Senate inactivity, and on occasion obstruction, is the source of some of the discontent. The work of the Senate is assumed by a few diligent senators and the House of Commons usually provides the Senate with little legislation until the end-of-session avalanche descends. The fact that the Senate is obliged to perform a major patronage function has not enhanced its prestige. Appointment to the Senate is considered a reward for those members of a political party who have served it loyally over the years. For many appointees the Senate is a convenient and well-paid exit from the political system. For others it is an advantageous site from which to manage election campaigns and raise party funds. The fact that senators have no direct responsibility to an electorate is a serious, though necessary, liability, but the use of the Senate to reward the devoted is the crucial weakness.

It has been suggested that the provinces nominate at least some members to the Senate in a manner similar to that used in the German Federal Republic for Laënder representation in the Bundesrat. In examining this proposal one should first consider the motives behind the idea. If it is stimulated by the belief that the appointment of those familiar with provincial interests will promote a higher quality of legislation, it should be viewed with suspicion. If, on the other hand, the suggestion is made in the hope that the Senate will be strengthened in the performance of integration, representation and legitimation functions, then there is justification for constructing elaborate representation formulas. In practical terms, the government does not require party stalwarts in the Senate and, as the current lack of partisanship indicates, there are possibilities for the development of regional and provincial loyalties if a different system of appointment is adopted. Offers of senatorships could also be extended to individuals in the arts and to other prominent Canadians who have had little or no prior association with politics. Major changes in composition would undoubtedly bring a re-evaluation of Senate activities. The future of the Senate lies not in the acquisition of more law-making functions, but in the improvement of its status as a symbol of the nation.

FORCES IN PARLIAMENT: GOVERNMENT AND OPPOSITION

If our knowledge of Parliament were confined to the formal procedures which govern law-making and surveillance in both houses, there would be a tendency to assume a mechanical view of this part of the legislative system. In reality Parliament does not react automatically and in a predetermined fashion to environmental pressures or even to the initiatives of the inner circle. Members of Parliament have individual goals which are often distinct from those held by interest groups or the bureaucracy. Some goals, such as the termination of a rail strike, involve conditions to be imposed on the environment; others, such as the restructuring of the parliamentary committee system, impose change on the House of Commons itself. In either case the formation of the goal may take place at the level of the individual (discussed in Chapter 7) or at the level of groups within Parliament.

The most important goals are those espoused by the parliamentary parties. Loyalty to a particular leadership means that on most occasions individual goals must be compromised so that group goals will have a possibility of success. The existence of cohesive parliamentary parties in Canada permits the government of the day to introduce and remain responsible for a legislative and financial program. It also makes individual behaviour relatively predictable, thus facilitating the establishment of norms which strengthen the parliamentary organization as a whole. In Chapter 3 we discussed how the organization of national parties has made them important participants in the political system. In Parliament their cohesion is attributable in part to the existence and regular functioning of caucus. As well as being a forum for the suggestion of policy changes, caucus is also a platform for the development of party strategy and an assembly where frustrations with the leadership may be aired. House leaders and party whips are also instrumental in the maintenance of party cohesion. They insure the party's voting strength at divisions (formal votes), decide on the order of parliamentary speakers, and are responsible for dispensing minor organization rewards and meting out criticism. In the face of pressures for party conformity, individual members of Parliament retain their personal goals, and often construct informal coalitions to secure the recognition of demands. But the overriding fact of parliamentary life is the existence of persistent and powerful political parties, and members of Parliament are encouraged to regard party cohesion as more important than freedom of action in the House.

Canadian parliamentary procedures are predicated on the existence of cohesive political parties, but the rules also recognize two aspects of parliamentary government: first, the existence of responsible government, which implies cabinet control over policy direction; and, secondly, the opportunity for opposition criticism of the government in Parliament.[17] These ideas command a high degree of support in Parliament and leaders and followers on both sides of the House are prepared to acknowledge their value and necessity.

Opposition to the policies of British monarchs was originally provided by the British Parliament as a whole. By the end of the eighteenth century a government had developed which was responsible to Parliament and it was possible for an opposition to exist without any overtones of treason. Instead of simply criticizing a king who could not be replaced, the opposition could now offer itself as the alternative government and political parties could be used to communicate parliamentary criticism to the public. The opposition thus became an institution of the British Parliament and in 1905 Canada became the first nation to officially recognize the position of Leader of Her Majesty's Loyal Opposition. In Canada, like Britain, the style of opposition which has emerged may be characterized as one of confrontation. Unlike presidential systems in which the executive and legislative branches rarely confront one another publicly, communication between the government and the opposition in Parliament is always direct. Criticism is a continuous and unavoidable aspect of a government's parliamentary experience and while the government must produce and defend a series of policies with at least implied goals, the opposition can content itself with one overriding goal—replacing the government. The confrontation style of opposition puts a premium on electoral success via parliamentary criticism, not on the changing of policy to suit party programs.

The confrontation style of opposition depends on the development of certain behavioural norms. On a general level, opposition members recognize the government's responsibility to carry on the business of governing and will often lend their support to that end while at the same time retaining for themselves the right to adequately criticize government policy. The government recognizes the opposition's right to criticize but denies it the right to obstruct. All governments attempt to anticipate opposition criticism and to formulate their strategy and tactics on the basis of this evaluation. Other norms have emerged to complement this arrangement. It is tacitly agreed, for example, that the government should refrain from introducing substantive amendments to legislation which has reached the committee stage of the parliamentary process. In June, 1973, when Solicitor General Warren Allmand attempted to introduce an amendment to a government bill on capital punishment during committee deliberations, his move was greeted with loud objections. When, on other occasions, the government considers there has been an excess of opposition obstruction, it applies the rules of the House to terminate debate. But, as both the government and the opposition recognize, it is more satisfactory to use the House leaders' meetings or informal discussions among party whips to negotiate the disposal of parliamentary time rather than force the issue to a division in the House of Commons where the government will normally emerge victorious.

The relationship between government and opposition in Canada is further complicated by frequent minority governments and by the different issues which emerge from the political environment. If a government is defined as an administration which assumes office after a general election or after a change in the Prime Minister, and a minority government as a situation in which the administration is controlled by a single party which lacks a plurality of votes in the House of Commons, then Canada has experienced more minority than majority governments since the end of the Second World War. Given the present party system and what appear to be stabilized levels of party support, minority situations will be a frequent outcome of federal elections in the future. When a minority government is in office the clearcut distinction between the government and the opposition disappears, as at least one opposition party is periodically called upon to lend its voting support to the government. Support is not offered for an indefinite period of time and under the threat of withdrawal governments have been led to stipulate that a defeat in the House will not be followed automatically by the government's resignation. John A. Macdonald was frequently defeated without resigning, and this traditional British practice was revived by the Pearson minority government in 1968. It suffered a defeat but tested the will of the House the following day on a formal nonconfidence motion. The fear of losing support has also led some Canadian prime ministers to seek the dissolution of Parliament before an election was constitutionally required. In 1926 Mackenzie King requested (and was denied) dissolution when it appeared his minority government was about to be defeated. Lester Pearson sought a majority with a premature election in 1965, as did Pierre Trudeau in 1968. Some prime ministers, Arthur Meighen in 1926, John Diefenbaker in 1963, and Trudeau in 1974 were forced to seek dissolution when support in the House of Commons was withdrawn.

Canadian governments are inclined to be impatient in minority situations. Research in foreign countries indicates that parties which are able to secure between 45 per cent and 50 per cent of the legislative seats (a condition in which minority governments in Canada have often found themselves), have an excellent chance of commanding the continual support of smaller parties.[18] Nevertheless, Canadian minority governments have often resorted to elections in their search for majority status. Apart from wartime arrangements, Canadian political parties have not experimented with coalitions which would, in effect, manufacture majorities. This mistrust of coalitions, inherited from Britain, contributes to a condition in which the membership of the smaller political parties is constantly denied the type of governmental experience that may generate voter confidence. However, the reluctance of opposition parties to enter coalition governments is not surprising. In Canada the dominant opposition style has emphasized that the goal of opposition parties is to establish themselves as viable alternatives, not as contributors to government policy.

It has been argued that the discomfort which accompanies minority status encourages a more responsive attitude in governments. Unfortunately, it is difficult to determine the validity of this argument although statistical indication of the impact of minority governments on legislative output is offered in chapter 8. Certainly there seems little dispute that the relationship between the opposition and the government becomes more complex and the government's ability to insist on coherent, comprehensive policy diminishes. Factors which were certainties for a majority government become imponderables. And the opposition, without sharing in the advantages of governing, also faces new intractable problems of internal cohesion and electoral strategy. After the 1972 election the New Democratic Party faced these difficulties when its caucus decided to extend its consistent support to the minority Liberal government.

Different issues force the opposition to adopt different styles.[10] Although the basic style is one of confrontation, some issues are of concern to only a few individuals in the legislative system. Such issues are usually debated by experts in the field. On such occasions an overly pugnacious opposition may violate the norms of government–opposition interaction and hinder the resolution of other issues on which the government and the opposition initially agree. In Canada many new issues defy categorization on the basis of traditional ideological divisions among parties. None of the political parties, for example, may call upon their philosophies for policies in the fields of consumer protection, pollution or low-income housing. Parties are forced to adopt positions on such issues, but the absence of historical precedents and ideological cues may provoke a splintered opposition and internal party dissension. During the 1973 debate on the Trudeau government's resolution on bilingualism in the public service, it was clear that agreement existed between the Prime Minister and the Leader of the Opposition on the basic content of the policy. However, the traditional Conservative response to the question of bilingualism had been ambiguous and Stanfield's commitment caused a break within the parliamentary party when the vote was taken. In this case a factional style of opposition replaced one of confrontation. The appearance of both factional and individualized opposition may increase if more opportunities are provided for members to acquire policy expertise and for groups within the party to develop policy views when there are no firm party commitments.

The Canadian parliamentary opposition faces persistent problems, regardless of the pattern of opposition that dominates at any one time. The most important of these is the difficulty opposition parties have experienced in achieving control of the government. There has been a tendency toward one-party dominance in Canada. The Liberals have held office for approximately three-quarters of the period since the Second World War. Electoral habits may have ossified to the degree that the three other parties are encouraged to consider themselves the permanent custodians of the opposition role. Perpetual opposition status makes it difficult to recruit qualified and attractive candidates and leads to frustrations among all opposition members of Parliament.

There seems to be a consensus among politicians (warranted or not) that a necessary condition of electoral success is a creditable performance in the House of Commons. It might be argued, therefore, that opposition problems can be traced to the government's domination of both parts of the legislative system and in particular to its ultimate control over the parliamentary timetable. The opposition has lost the right to "talk out" government bills (closure, 1913), to filibuster (a limit on individual debate, 1927), to extend indefinitely major debates (1955), and to appeal the rulings of the Speaker (1965). But procedural changes have been slow and methodical and there is agreement, even among members of the opposition, that tactics that may once have been considered legitimate modes of criticism are now undeniably instruments of obstruction. Even the complaint that the opposition lacks the research facilities to conduct a critical campaign in the House has been partly met. In 1969 Parliament allocated $195,000 to research assistance for all opposition parties and by 1972 this had risen to over one-third of a million dollars. Furthermore, the opposition as a whole is granted, on a continual basis, large blocks of time during which it assumes responsibility for the initiation of debate in the House. It is the backbencher, not the opposition, who has lost the battle for parliamentary time.

If the government is unable to secure the passage of legislation in a suitable period, the House rules provide two opportunities to circumvent parliamentary opposition by the termination of debate. These rules are not only difficult to apply, but their persistent use violates the norms of government–opposition relations. The most notorious procedure is closure. Introduced in 1913, it is a weapon which governments impose only reluctantly because of the adverse political ramifications. In addition, various procedural conditions must be met before it can be employed. Closure must be moved on individual clauses, not on an entire bill, and in the case of bills with many clauses the attractiveness of closure fades appreciably. Notice of the intention to use closure must be given at a previous sitting and before closure may be moved debate on a clause must have been adjourned or consideration of it "postponed." To be postponed, a clause must have been discussed. During the pipeline debate of 1956, C. D. Howe was forced to introduce the first clause of the bill, speak to it briefly to satisfy procedural requirements, and then move that it be postponed, a tactic which attracted violent objections from the opposition. Even if the procedural conditions can be satisfied, closure only applies to the particular stage at which it is moved. Until the 30th Parliament it has been used on only eight bills since 1913 and on every occasion acrimonious debate ensued.

In 1969 the government introduced, and had to use closure to pass, a complicated standing order which provided a formal basis for the negotiated settlement of time disputes in the House. The rules provide that if all of the parties (in the case of Standing Order 75A), or a majority of the parties (in the case of 75B), or two, but possibly one, of the parties (in the case of 75C), can agree, a particular amount of time will be allotted to the consideration of a particular stage of a bill. Unfortunately, sloppy drafting has turned a useful set of rules into an unwieldy and unpredictable procedure. The rules have often been considered a continuum with the parties obliged to seek agreement under 75A first, then 75B, and finally 75C, but there is some doubt that 75B is a necessary step. There is even the possibility that a majority of the opposition parties may agree, under 75B, to an allocation which a majority government is forced to accept. Since the imposition of 75A implies unanimous party approval, the requirements for its introduction are not particularly stringent. No notice of motion is needed, the allocation for more than one stage may be moved at once, and no amendments or debate is allowed. The moving of 75B requires no notice, but debate can take place for a maximum of two hours. More stringent rules apply to 75C including a notice of motion, a debate on the motion, a provision for amendments, separate motions for each stage, and at least one day's debate at each stage before the motion can be presented to the House. Since invoking time allocation may require as much time as the normal process of debate, the government must be committed to a fixed deadline as it was on the 1972 tax bill, the most important legislation on which time allocation has been employed.

Our contention is that opposition criticism has not been stifled in the House by procedural innovations, but that opposition difficulties are traceable to more fundamental problems which, in some cases, apply to parliamentary oppositions in other countries. One of the problems is that much of the most articulate and publicized criticism of government policy does not originate with the opposition in Parliament but with other structures in the political environment. Interest groups, in particular, too often provide the major reactions and criticisms to government proposals. The government has also established quasi-independent agencies such as the Economic Council of Canada and provided them with resources and experts that outweigh those of the opposition in the House of Commons. Such bodies represent a highly competitive source of ideas and criticism, and are often accorded more attention by the press than specific opposition criticisms in Parliament. The familiar argument that the Canadian provinces provide the effective political opposition also deserves serious consideration in this context. Voters may not choose provincial governments on these grounds but there is little doubt that the clashes between the provinces and the federal government at intergovernmental conferences detract attention from the federal parliamentary opposition on some of the most important issues in Canadian politics. Increased opportunities for parliamentary surveillance of all federal-provincial conferences would strengthen the role of federal politicians, and particularly the opposition, in the legislative system.

It is often difficult for oppositions to offer major policy alternatives. By lending support to the regime and the accepted norms of government, the Canadian parliamentary opposition is unable to reflect certain forms of dissent in society. The opposition endorses only legitimate means of political expression. This is not the case in France and Italy, for example, where the parliamentary opposition reflects an array of ideologies aimed at reconstituting the regime and/or the social structure. Moreover, not all issues evoke automatic responses from opposition parties. With the achievement of the welfare state and a mixed economy, ideological disputes in North America seem to have given way to a search for policy consensus. Parliamentary oppositions are encouraged to criticize the specifics of government policy rather than develop comprehensive policy alternatives. The opposition usually represents an alternative source of individuals, not ideas.

In the Canadian legislative system, opposition activities ought to contribute to the system's capacity to perform its diverse functions. In a country where there are alternating governments, the parliamentary opposition may perform a vital recruitment function by providing an experienced political elite equipped to assume political office. The dominance of a single political party in Canada has diminished the opposition's capacity to aid in the performance of this function. In a political system dominated by linguistic, cultural, and regional cleavages the existence of a legitimate and representative parliamentary opposition might help to integrate the political system. However, the reasonably high level of fragmentation in the Canadian political culture makes it difficult for opposition parties to span all the important political cleavages. The fact that the opposition freely participates in parliamentary rituals and demonstrates a commitment to legal procedures should enhance Parliament's ability to perform a legitimation function. When criticism is publicized it creates the impression that there is little need for an extra-parliamentary opposition. In Canada this function is performed reasonably well, but institutional change could enhance the salience of the opposition and thereby improve the status of Parliament as a whole.

An adequate execution of ascribed functions depends on the opposition's capacity to offer comprehensive critiques and detailed amendments of government policy. However, as the pressure on parliamentary time increases, it becomes more difficult to create an atmosphere on the floor of the House in which both general and detailed criticism can be accommodated. The committees ought to develop into workshops where members can appreciate and criticize the most intricate and technical of legislative proposals. A relaxation of administrative secrecy and the provision of more professional advice to members of Parliament are required. Moreover, in the committee forum, government and opposition members should interact under a different set of norms than those prescribed by the confrontation style of opposition. Since the introduction of the new committee system in 1968, there are signs that such a development is under way. It is an extension, not a reversal of this trend, that would alleviate some of the problems in the legislative system.

NOTES

1. Canadian Institute of Public Opinion, December 1964. For a summary of similar evidence, see Allan Kornberg, "Parliament in Canadian Society," in Allan Kornberg and Lloyd D. Musolf, eds., *Legislatures in Developmental Perspective* (Durham: Duke University Press, 1970), pp. 55-128.
2. In this book we shall not attempt to discuss all the procedures of the House or the role of parliamentary officials. For a comprehensive, although somewhat dated review, see W. F. Dawson, *Procedure in the Canadian House of Commons* (Toronto: University of Toronto Press, 1962).
3. T. A. Hockin, "The Advance of Standing Committees in

Canada's House of Commons: 1965 to 1970," *Canadian Public Administration*, Vol. 13, no. 2 (Summer 1970), pp. 185-202.

4. Colin Campbell, "Institutional Modernization in a Parliamentary System: The Canadian Senate," a paper prepared for the Canadian Political Science Association, Toronto, June 1974, pp. 15-16.
5. For a study of the Public Accounts Committee, see Norman Ward, *The Public Purse* (Toronto: University of Toronto Press, 1962).
6. Between 1955 and 1962 Canada experimented unsuccessfully with an Estimates Committee comprised of sixty members of the House. See Norman Ward, "The Committee on Estimates," *Canadian Public Administration*, Vol. 6, no. 1 (March 1963), pp. 35-42.
7. The procedures with respect to supplementary estimates are different. These may be referred to standing committees at any time, as Standing Order 58 (15) provides only that "supplementary estimates shall be referred to a standing committee . . . immediately they are presented in the House." However, the standing committees are required to report the estimates back to the House not later than three sitting days before the final sitting or the last allotted day in the supply period in which they are referred. If the committees do not comply, the estimates will be deemed to have been reported by that date. Consequently, standing committees could theoretically be given as little as one day to report supplementary estimates.
8. See the statement by the Hon. E. Benson reported in *The Parliamentarian*, Vol. 49 (1968), p. 36.
9. Of course, not all executive power is delegated by Parliament. For a discussion of prerogative power see Mallory, *The Structure of Canadian Government*, pp. 137-146.
10. John Kersell, *Parliamentary Supervision of Delegated Legislation* (London: Stevens and Sons Co., 1960).
11. Canada, House of Commons, Special Committee on Statutory Instruments, *Third Report* (Ottawa, 1969).
12. Six of the motions may be non-confidence motions, two within each period. The periods include five days to be used before December 10, seven before March 26, and thirteen before June 30.
13. *Confederation Debates*, 1865, p. 571.
14. Ibid., p. 36.
15. Ibid.
16. R. A. MacKay, *The Unreformed Senate of Canada*, revised ed. (Toronto: McClelland and Stewart, 1963), p. 9.
17. Few studies have been made of the opposition in Canada. For an overview, see Thomas Hockin, "Adversary Politics and Some

Functions of the Canadian House of Commons" in Kruhlak *et al., The Political Process in Canada*, pp. 361-381.

18. Valentine Herman and John Pope, "Minority Governments in Western Democracies," *British Journal of Political Science*, Vol. 3 (April 1973), pp. 191-212.
19. For an extended discussion see Andrew J. Milnor and Mark N. Franklin, "Patterns of Opposition Behaviour in Modern Legislatures" in Allan Kornberg, ed., *Legislatures in Comparative Perspective* (New York: David McKay, 1973), pp. 421-446.

6. Parliament II: The Standing Committee System

The Canadian Parliament divides into committees in an attempt to perform its functions with as much efficiency as possible.[1] Theoretically, committees furnish institutions with a high level of performance because they allow the workload to be shared among specialized personnel. Committees of the House of Commons, however, have been used for additional purposes and their structures are the confused product of a series of compromises between several competing points of view about their role in the system. The committees have not yet developed to their full potential, and institutional change in this sector of Parliament could provide additional opportunities for individual participation in the policy-making process and possibly an improvement in the performance of the legislature.

There is an assumption, common among Canadian parliamentarians, that there are only two models of committee activity for a legislature. This idea is usually expressed in the contention that, given their present direction, Canadian committees will soon resemble those of the American Congress. The evidence for this view is the increasing activity of committees and what many individuals interpret as indications of their growing independence from the House and the government. What seems to guide this notion is the erroneous impression that the increased activity and independence of committees can only lead away from a parliamentary government and toward some variation of the American congressional system. But this represents only one of a multitude of possibilities.

The inadequacy of a formal-legal view may be demonstrated by a comparative examination of committee systems. The most important relationship is the one that committees maintain with their parent body. Committee autonomy or dependence is always a matter of degree, as all committee systems are controlled by their legislatures to a certain extent. In Canada and the United Kingdom, for example, they can act only when given a reference and the legislature acts on committee advice only through a report. In the United States, where committees are more independent, bills and all other matters may still be forced out of committee by a discharge petition signed by a majority of members of the House of Representatives. In some committee systems members are actually empowered to write legislation and this undertaking is not confined to the congressional model of government. In the parliamentary systems of Italy and the defunct Fourth French Republic, deputies actually wrote laws in committees, whereas in Canada and Britain committees are used merely to "tidy up" legislation. In short, constitutional forms are not the sole determinate of committee activity.

Extensive research facilities are also regarded as the hallmarks of a congressional committee system. In the United States, the professional research staff serves the needs of the entire committee as well as the leadership. However, in some congressional systems, such as the Philippines, the research staff is hired for the committee but only works for the chairman. When such a chairman loses his position, he takes the staff with him. In the United Kingdom some of the select committees have had researchers for dealing with difficult subject matter. While no specific staff is provided for committees in Canada, the Research Branch of the Parliamentary Library is prepared to aid committees and ad hoc arrangements are often made for important committee deliberations. In other words, in some countries the staff works for the whole committee, in some countries it works for the chairman, and in others ad hoc arrangements are made. But in all countries, at least some attempt is made to provide staff for committees. The fact that staff is provided is not symptomatic of inaugurating a congressional committee system.

In Canada there is no generally accepted model for committee activity. No consensus has emerged on questions of independence and partisanship in internal committee proceedings. In majority situations the opposition is less interested in the committee system than is the government. At committee meetings the attendance record of opposition parties on a proportional basis has continually fallen below that of government members. The attitude of the opposition epitomizes one that, until recently, was prevalent among most backbenchers in Great Britain. According to this view, the real forum for debate ought to be the floor of the House of Commons, and any attempt to increase the role of the committees will be at the expense of the House. In contrast to the opposition, government backbenchers seem to cherish the independence which the committee system provides. The committee system allows an outlet for government members who are deprived of opportunities to speak frequently in the House. Furthermore, in majority situations, government backbenchers have control of the process, since their members constitute a majority on every committee.

At present, the standing (permanent) committee system is based only on the organizational principle that committees should be multi-functional. Most committees are expected to legislate, scrutinize, advise and investigate. A committee may pass clauses of a bill (legislate) and at the same time gather information (investigate). But this basic organizational arrangement is not founded on a clear conception either of the relations which ought to prevail between the House and its committees or of the parliamentary model to which Canada should aspire.

DISCONTINUITIES IN THE DEVELOPMENT OF THE COMMITTEE SYSTEM

At Confederation Canada adopted a weak standing committee system. The committees were designed to parallel government departments and, in much the same way that the government has reorganized its departmental structure, committees have changed to keep pace with changes in specialization. But until recently they remained generalist committees. They were often inactive and performed whatever task the House assigned to them during the course of a session.

Since Confederation there has been some pressure to increase the number of committees. In 1867 there were ten committees, in 1945, fifteen committees and by 1965, twenty-one standing committees were in operation. In the nineteenth century the size of the committees fluctuated, but since the session of 1910–11 there has been a general decrease. In 1907 one committee had nearly two hundred members and two had 125, but from 1927 to 1964 the largest committee had sixty members while most had thirty-five or less.

Academic critics of this system condemned the unwieldy size of committees, the lack of truly specialist committees with expert members, and the practice of electing excessively partisan chairmen. Some of these criticisms were heeded, but until the early 1960s reform of the committee system remained a topic incidental to reform of procedures in Parliament itself. The old committee system was based on the premise that the floor of the House was the centre of significant parliamentary activity.

From Confederation until 1962 there were only six major overhauls of the procedures of the House. Since then there have been noteworthy changes in 1962, 1964, 1965, 1968 and 1969. Not all of them have been directed specifically at the committee system, but most have had at least some effect in this area. As early as the 26th Parliament some committees were beginning to play a considerable role in the system. The Defence committee, in particular, broke new ground by both travelling abroad and by examining the minister and a large number of officials and defence experts.

It was not until 1965, however, that a spirit of reform overtook what has been called the old committee system. The Special Committee on Procedure, which had been constituted to suggest reforms in the parliamentary process, took a keen interest in the committee system itself. Through the work of that committee the old list of standing committees was drastically revised, and the membership on an average committee substantially reduced. The House also agreed in 1965 to make greater use of standing committees for the detailed examination of legislation and public spending. Throughout the 27th Parliament more departmental estimates were referred to standing committees and, as never before, public servants and MPs were brought into direct and continuous contact.

In 1968 and 1969 the provisional reforms of 1965 were consolidated and some additional important reforms introduced. While these changes may appear to be the culmination of an unbroken movement for reform in the committee system, this view is not entirely accurate. The Special Committee on Procedure (1967–68), which initiated these final changes, was more interested in improving proceedings in the chamber than in the committee system. It decided that the Committee of Supply, the Committee of Ways and Means and the Committee of the Whole House, were too cumbersome and inefficient to handle the increased volume and complexity of legislation and public spending. The operations of the standing committee system were not reviewed extensively and those changes that were made were designed essentially to expedite proceedings in the House.

In the new system all bills were to be referred to the appropriate standing committees for clause-by-clause study after the second reading unless the House specified otherwise. Only bills based on a Supply or a Ways and Means motion continued to be referred to the Committee of the Whole. Thus, use of the Committee of the Whole was drastically curtailed and this enhanced the role of standing committees in studying legislation. It was hoped that debate at report stage would not repeat detailed debate in committee.

Departmental estimates were referred to an appropriate standing committee for detailed study. Simultaneously the Committee of Supply was abolished, making the standing committee system the important forum for the scrutiny of government spending. The main estimates were to be tabled normally in February, allowing approximately three months for detailed examination by committees after which they were automatically deemed reported to the House. In addition to the scrutinizing function, it was hoped that standing committees would become familiar with the estimates and through them the operations of the departments and agencies examined. The result was an overall increase in time devoted to estimates and related activities and some relief to the timetable of the House. In order to compensate the opposition for the abolition of the Committee of Supply, twenty-five days were allotted over three separate "supply periods" during which the opposition could choose the topics for discussion.

During this same period the Committees Branch, which provides technical support, underwent an evolution. Shorthand reporting was phased out and electronic recording of committee proceedings was phased in. Efforts were made to speed up the production of committee reports and, for the first time, to produce reports in French concurrently. The result was a substantial increase in the staff of the Committees Branch used for transcribing, editing, translating and recording.

At the time of these procedural amendments it would have been worthwhile to have undertaken a complete examination of the committee system itself. However, this option was not chosen and the committee system which had been in operation since 1965 was reconstituted with only minor changes. The new committee system was therefore the product of a tremendous increase in duties and responsibilities, but procedures and functions were not made congruent with the entire legislative process.

The 1968 rule changes have not resolved disagreements about the direction of committee evolution. Tension continues between the attitudes of government and opposition backbenchers. There is also some concern that power may flow from the generalized floor to the specialized committees (with their restricted membership) and diminish the grandeur of performance in the House. As a result, committees rarely conduct their own appraisals of social problems. They remain totally dependent on outside resources and have difficulty initiating new ideas. On the rare occasion when there is committee publicity some members worry that the public's interest is transferred away from the House of Commons.

There have also been technical irritants in the committee system because it was reformed without being properly integrated into the general legislative process.

(a) Management problems have arisen because of a lack of coordination of the activities of the committees and the House.

(b) The procedural devices for linking the House to its committees, namely references, reports and concurrence, were developed before the new committee system and have not been changed to correspond to the innovations.
(c) Because of the new responsibilities committees have assumed in the legislative process there are problems in their size and membership.
(d) The leadership roles within committees, namely the chairmen, parliamentary secretaries and ministers, have not been made congruent with the responsibilities of the new committee system.
(e) Procedures within committees have been left unspecified and while this caused little difficulty in the old system, the omission has had a detrimental effect in the new one.
(f) Committee travelling and the calling of witnesses have not been organized with sufficient care to avoid management problems.
(g) There is too great a burden of work for committees at particular times of the year.

COMMITTEE STRUCTURE AND ACTIVITIES

The role of Common's standing committees in law-making and surveillance was discussed in chapter 5. In order to assess the problems in the new committee system this chapter examines the committees' relations with the House, its activities, its leadership and the staff which support its operation. Attention to the minutiae is not always illuminating, but in the case of these microcosms of the House, the resolution of problems is to be discovered both in a general assessment of performance and in an appreciation of the procedural and behavioural details which structure the activities of the committee system.

a. House and Committee Interaction

Provision is made in the Standing Orders of the House of Commons for eighteen specific standing committees: Agriculture and External Affairs and National Defence may have no more than thirty members; Procedure and Organization may have no more than twelve members; and the remainder may have no more than twenty members in each committee. The membership of any special committee is limited by Standing Order 65 (5) to no more than fifteen. Unlike the standing committees, these special committees exist only during the session in which they are appointed, after which they must be renewed or they automatically expire. There are also special joint and standing joint committees which include members of both the House and Senate.

Since committees are extensions of the House they must be linked to it for both constitutional and practical purposes. The procedural devices of references, reports, and motions of concurrence accomplish this task. Committees cannot operate unless their activities are specified in the standing orders or they receive a reference from the House instructing them to pursue a particular topic. Orders of reference are debatable, and while most originate with the government the opposition may also suggest that particular subjects be referred to committee. Government agreement in such cases is rare but not unknown. In 1970 the Biafran crisis was referred to a Commons committee on a motion from the opposition leader, Robert Stanfield.

While committees may consider only those topics which have been referred to them by the House, their members are inclined to ignore the specific terms of their references and to expand them whenever possible. In some cases the government and Parliament have tacitly permitted a committee chairman to expand a committee reference by interpretation. For example, on April 29, 1970, the Standing Committee on Fisheries and Forestry added to their report on departmental estimates a rider which underlined the inadequacies of fisheries research and suggested the provision of additional funds. On occasion there have been suggestions that committees should be punished because they have expanded their references by interpretation. Some members believed, for example, that the External Affairs and National Defence committee should not have received another general reference in the 28th Parliament because its report on Canadian-American relations went beyond the committee's reference. Others believed that in practical terms the general reference of the government's foreign policy papers allowed the committee to examine any issue on this broad topic.

The standing orders declare that committees have the power "to report from time to time." When committees conclude their deliberations reports are tabled and a motion for concurrence is in order. However, procedural wrangles continue to detract from the importance of this link between committees and the House. Except in the case of bills, there are different views about the significance of concurrence (or agreement) in a committee report. Concurrence may be moved on what might be called "substantive" reports which make policy recommendations and on "housekeeping" reports which request, for example, the right to travel or engage staff. A large percentage of substantive reports do not receive concurrence from the House, but the government still implements their contents. On the other hand, some substantive reports receive concurrence but no government action. The government is reluctant to have concurrence moved on substantive reports for two reasons. First, since the motions are debatable, they consume House time without necessarily enhancing publicity for the report itself. Secondly, the status of a report which has obtained concurrence is ambiguous. As in other House proceedings, it is necessary to determine if a motion for concurrence is an order of the House or a statement of opinion. Orders are binding on the officers and servants of Parliament; a second reading motion, for example, is an order to the Table to read the bill. Resolutions, on the other hand, are the opinions of the House; they may have political ramifications but they are not law. Parliamentarians are divided over the "real meaning" of concurrence in substantive reports and what they wish this procedure to accomplish.

There has also been disagreement on who may move motions of concurrence. Because of a Speaker's ruling, the opportunity now exists for any member to move a motion of concurrence during Routine Proceedings of the House.[2] This has had the effect of eroding an institutionalized link in the system. In accordance with the thesis that the chairman is the individual who links the House and the committee (he signs the report), it seems reasonable that only he, on the expressed authority of the committee, should be allowed to move concurrence.

A report is the only instrument which will force the House to recognize the collective views of the committee membership. Some members have attempted to use the reports of committees to give expression to personal opinions. However, minority reports are not considered procedurally valid. In rejecting the tabling of a minority report to the main report of the Special Joint Committee on the Constitution on March 16, 1972, the Speaker declared that this practice is "unknown" in Canadian and British experience. On occasion minority ideas have been appended or smuggled into the text of a report. This has caused some interesting and amusing anomalies. In the report on the Canadian flag every affirmative and negative vote was recorded. In a report from External Affairs and National Defence on NATO, a lack of unanimity was suggested in several places. At least one of the authors was quite pleased that his minority ideas had been smuggled into the main body of the study.

There are arguments for and against the inclusion of minority reports in a formalized way. The basic argument in favour is that they allow backbenchers to have an input into the report even when they disagree with the majority opinion in the committee. This technique is desirable from the point of view of participation, since it increases information sent to the House and the public about the views of individual members. On the other hand, there are several disadvantages. Such a proposal might discourage members from reaching a consensus, and every report might be divided into a majority report which expressed the government's views and a minority report which expressed the views of the opposition. Moreover if it became the usual practice that members other than the chairmen could move concurrence or that minority reports were acceptable, a majority government might be tempted to deny references to committees or to instruct its majority not to produce a report at all.

The primary object of a committee report is to influence government policy. However, departments regard committee reports as less significant than those from royal commissions or task forces. In the formative stages of policy-making, influence flows from departments to committees rather than from politicians to bureaucrats. The government does not even bother to explain why it has been unable to accept committee recommendations, regardless of whether or not they have received concurrence. In Australia, on the other hand, committee reports continually provide the basis for debates in the House of Commons. In Canada a procedure to trigger automatic debate of committee reports is required and proposals to stimulate such House and committee interaction will be offered in the last chapter.

b. Committee Membership and Deliberations

The success of committees in the legislative system is influenced by the same dynamics that affect all small groups. Among the topics treated by group theorists are the size of groups, their membership turnover, and the length of their meetings. Although it appears that, for better or for worse, parliamentary institutions in Canada have still to utilize some of the innovative techniques of modern management, there exists a preponderance of concern for the issues of committee size and membership. In fact, manipulation of committee size and membership may be a feasible means of improving the performance and the smooth operation of the committee system.

As discussed earlier, the movement toward more committees with smaller memberships has been going on since the nineteenth century. The 1965 provisional committee system and the new system of 1968 have continued this trend. While the total membership in all committees in 1965 was lowered by only 46, the average membership per committee dropped from 40.8 members to 25.0 because seven extra standing committees were attached to the system. As Table 1 shows, the average number of committees to which a member can presently belong is less than two. The system expanded in terms of the number of standing committees, but the notion that committees ought to be large enough to accommodate the general interests of all members was abandoned. If committees were to perform specialized functions and to acquire more expertise among individual members, they could not be burdened with a mass membership.

The allotment of positions on committees to the various parties is determined by a consideration of party strength in the House and other norms about proper parliamentary organization. In a majority situation, no government party will accept

Table 1: SIZE AND MEMBERSHIP OF STANDING COMMITTEES, 1960-1972

Session	Number of standing committees[1]	Total membership	Average membership per committee	Number of committees per average eligible member
1960	14	571	40.8	2.4
1960-61	14	571	40.8	2.4
1962	14	571	40.8	2.4
1962-63	13	536	41.2	2.3
1963	13	571	40.8	2.4
1964-65	14	571	40.8	2.4
1965	21	525	25.0	2.2
1966-67	21	525	25.0	2.2
1967-68	21	525	25.0	2.2
1968-69	18	364	20.2	1.6
1969-70	18	376	20.9	1.6
1970-71-72	18	376	20.9	1.6
1972	18	376	20.9	1.6

SOURCE: *Journals of the House of Commons.*

[1]Does not include joint standing committees

less than 50 per cent of the members of each committee. The weakest party is not denied representation on any committee and the official opposition usually insists on special privileges. Despite the obvious difficulties the proportionality rule is faithfully applied even during minority governments. In both cases the party leadership determines which individuals will be assigned to each committee but requests can usually be accommodated. Members tend to choose committees whose subject matter accords with their professional training or constituency interests.

The new committee system has been marked by more activity. The number of committee meetings increased from

Graph 1: ATTENDANCE PATTERN AT STANDING COMMITTEES IN THE SECOND SESSION OF THE 28TH PARLIAMENT

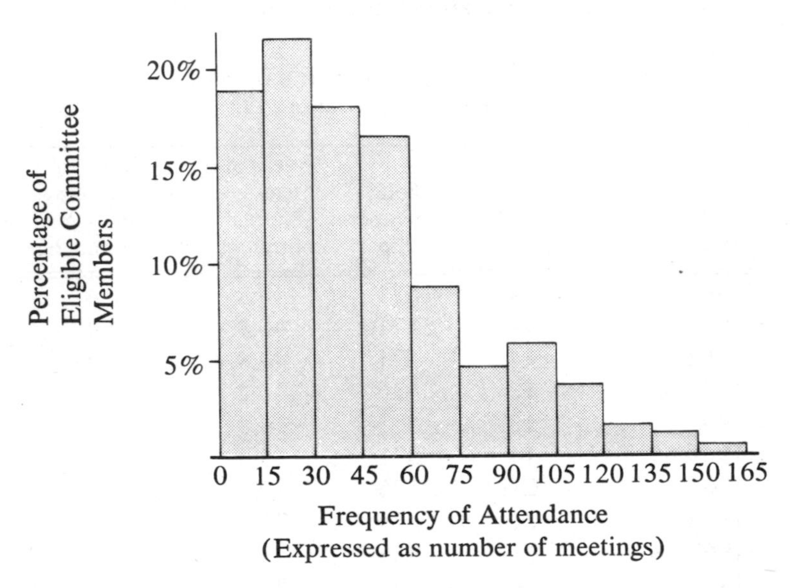

SOURCE: *Proceedings of the Standing Committees.*

218 in the second session of the 27th Parliament to 759 in the second session of the 28th Parliament. In the same period registered attendances increased from 3,105 to 9,909 (see Table 2). Devotion to committee duties, however, has not been shown equally by all members. Graph I indicates that for the latter session, 40 per cent of those eligible for committees attended no more than thirty meetings. With well over seven hundred committee meetings to be manned it is quite clear that the burden was not equally distributed. One indefatigable member attended over 150 meetings. It is also worth noting that not all parties contribute equally to the functioning of the committee system. In the second session of the 28th Parliament members of the Liberal party met 74 per cent of their total opportunities for attendance, the Progressive Conservative party met 55.5 per cent of their opportunities, the NDP 68 per cent and the Créditistes 21 per cent.

Attendance at meetings varies from committee to committee.

In the second session of the 28th Parliament the average attendance ranged from a low of 8.2 in the case of the Miscellaneous Estimates Committee to a high of 15.5 in the case of the Transport and Communications Committee, with an average attendance for all the twenty-member committees of 11.2 members. The figure for average attendance of committee members at meetings during which bills were discussed was 12.9 members per meeting. This discrepancy may indicate that the interest of members in discussing bills was higher than their interest in discussing estimates or the subject matter of general references.

Table 2: COMPARISON OF COMMITTEE ACTIVITIES*

	2nd Session 27th Parliament	2nd Session 28th Parliament
Total number of committee meetings	218	759
Total number of attendances registered by MPs	3,105	9,909
Total number of attendances recorded by officials	490	999
Total number of attendances recorded by witnesses	323	885
Total number of attendances recorded by members as observers	103	690

SOURCE: *Proceedings of the Standing Committees.*
*Each session consisted of 155 days.

The Chief Government Whip is responsible for changing committee membership and all that is required is a notification authorized by his office. Prior to the 1968 rule changes the procedure for shuffling membership was more rigid. A motion had to be introduced and concurred in while the House was sitting in order to accomplish a membership change. The new rules have naturally led to a great fluidity in committee membership. Statistics reveal that for all the committee meetings held during the second session of the 28th Parliament, there was a total of 2,627 membership substitutions; the average rate of substitution was therefore 2.4 members per meeting.

According to the philosophy of the Special Committee on Procedure which brought in the new rules, members were to develop more expertise in the subject matter of their committees. Establishing continuity in the membership was to contribute to this objective. However, the ease with which members are moved from committee to committee in the new system effectively thwarts continuous membership. The efficacy and even legitimacy of committee work is jeopardized as a result of heavy membership turnover. Members often move in and out of committee meetings with such facility that the meeting itself is disrupted. Although it is not a violation of the rules, many believe that the practice of inserting groups of MPs into committee proceedings for the sole purpose of carrying votes illustrates contempt for the entire process of committee discussion and voting.

Committees, like most organizations, experience peak periods of operation. Seldom does business flow so smoothly that activity is kept at a constant level. The period of heavy activity begins in February with the referral of estimates to standing committees and ends in May with their return to the House. During the second session of the 28th Parliament, between February and May, the average number of committee meetings per month was 111. The average number of meetings per month during the remainder of the session was 38. The effectiveness of any organization or system is severely compromised by such major fluctuations in activity. During a busy period in committee, members are still required on the floor of the House of Commons. Where no special arrangements are made to cope with the extra burden of work some items of business may be given less than proper attention.

The efficient organization of this vast amount of committee activity requires the coordination of government, House and committee business. Since 1968 committees have been consuming a greater portion of members' time but the government has experienced difficulty in imposing a schedule of committee meetings because of the fear of treading on the tradition of committee independence. As a result members are often required to attend two or more meetings at the same time. For example, in May 1971 the actual incidence of individual membership conflict was 294. To alleviate these difficulties the government ought to make its legislative program and its intentions known farther in advance and committee chairmen should plan more thoroughly the business of their committees. These reforms should be accompanied by a rigorous adherence to a system of committee scheduling and the requirement that committee membership changes be strictly limited.

The increased volume of committee deliberations is attributable, in part, to the responsibilities committees have assumed for the scrutiny of legislation and estimates. The new committee system has also provided members with many more opportunities to conduct general investigations. Perhaps the most celebrated of committee studies was the review of the White Paper on Tax Reform conducted by the Standing Committee on Finance and Economic Affairs. Some committees continually conduct investigations. In the 28th Parliament the Standing Committee on External Affairs and National Defence, which receives very little legislation, considered both the "Foreign Policy for Canadians" papers and the White Paper entitled "Defence in the 70s." Much to the discomfort of the government this committee also recommended 51 per cent Canadian ownership of foreign industry. In the 29th Parliament it reviewed the government's position on the Third Conference on the Law of the Sea and the subject of the Inter-parliamentary Conference on European Integration. When given the opportunity, committees also respond to specific demands. In May 1972 the question of rail passenger service in southern Ontario was referred to the Standing Committee on Transportation and Communication. The committee visited several cities in the province, heard sixty-eight witnesses, received fifty-five briefs in addition to petitions and letters, and finally recommended that all discontinued passenger service be restored.

On occasion, committees receive general investigatory references instead of specific bills on the same subjects. In November 1973 the Standing Committee on Justice and Legal Affairs began consideration of the subject matter of a new national holiday instead of the three private members' bills that had initiated consideration of the question. Even when bills are sent to committees the subject matter may also be referred, as illustrated by the case of tobacco advertising in the 28th Parliament. But investigatory references are not given only to aid the committees. The government may attempt to use the committee system as a forum to solicit public response to proposals, as in the case of the White Paper on Tax Reform, or even to delay consideration of an item, as with the creation of the Special Committee on Drug Costs and Prices in the 27th Parliament. Committee investigation may also be a convenient way of employing the energies of those backbenchers restless for a larger role in policy-making.

In all of their internal deliberations committees endeavour to establish links with the political environment and the inner circle. They hear witnesses both to obtain expert opinions and to acquaint themselves with competing points of view on the issues under consideration. The power to summon and examine witnesses in standing committees derives from the Senate and House of Commons Act. On subjects of a technical or private nature the usual practice has been to summon those directly involved. In such cases committee members are usually well informed and can compile an extensive list of witnesses. On matters of wide public interest most witnesses request to be heard, and the chairman or the steering committee acts as a screening device. The vast majority of witnesses appear on behalf of groups who either have a special interest in the matter at hand, or who make it a general policy to keep in touch with committees and present briefs on various occasions.

The attendance rate of departmental officials at committee hearings has been increasing. Officials made 490 appearances in committees during the second session of the 27th Parliament and 999 in the second session of the 28th Parliament; this has undoubtedly placed pressure on the workload of senior public servants. The attendance of non-departmental witnesses has also increased. In the earlier session 323 appearances were made and this rose to 885 in the second session of the 28th Parliament. As might be expected with the revitalized committee system, witnesses appeared more often on bills than they had before, but the largest increase was the attendance on miscellaneous items. In the second session of the 28th Parliament, 61 per cent of committee time was devoted to miscellaneous items which included annual reports, white papers and general investigatory references. In the second session of the 27th Parliament only 32 per cent of committee time was spent on these matters. Witnesses were on hand on 129 occasions for these topics in the earlier session and 514 occasions in the later session. The new committee system has established stronger lines of communication with interested publics and has expanded this network through more committees and into more subject areas than ever before.

Apart from the technical problems which the committee system must face in its practices concerning witnesses, there are two general questions which should be posed. First, how can the committee system best regulate the appearance of witnesses to ensure that their contributions and, through them, the contributions of committees, receive the widest possible hearing and make the greatest possible impact in the legislative system? Secondly, how can the committee system ensure that it hears a representative cross-section of opinion on matters of importance? The present practice of committees suggests that Parliament has no general policy with regard to either of these questions.

Since the most important decisions on legislation are taken long before committees examine bills, witnesses have little impact except that which comes through educating members and establishing parliamentary contacts. In majority situations very few substantive amendments are made in committee without the prior consent or cooperation of the government. Unless it is the hope of witnesses to influence the details and the technical wording of legislation then much of their time is wasted. If witnesses are to have a more significant impact on policy formation then committees must have an input earlier in the legislative process. A related difficulty is the extent to which witnesses accurately represent the range of opinion in the country. Some subjects are specialized and concern only a few individuals, most of whom are present or represented. Other subjects, especially those being handled at the level of a white paper, are of general interest and the assumption that all views are heard is probably unfounded. The witnesses in attendance and the briefs prepared are usually on behalf of interested groups and very seldom on behalf of individuals. This simple fact suggests that those groups which maintain a continuous organization are in a more advantageous position to affect parliamentary decisions than those groups or individuals who do not. It is by no means certain, for example, that the Standing Committee on Finance and Economic Affairs considered in a sophisticated fashion how to select which groups and individuals to hear out of the more than one thousand who wished to comment on the White Paper on Tax Reform. Moreover, the present system does not ensure that the unorganized and the poor, for example, will have their views argued before committees.

Another perplexing problem faced by committees in their deliberations involves the protection afforded to witnesses. The protections derive both from general law and from the practices and procedures of Parliament. Even though the rules are designed to protect witnesses, the committee system has experienced difficulties recently which serve to cast doubt on their efficacy. In the first place, it seems reasonably clear that most witnesses are unaware of their rights and avenues of appeal or that they may claim the protection of the Canada Evidence Act if they feel their testimony might be self-incriminating. Secondly, witnesses who have been damaged by unfair criticism in a committee report do not have a remedy before the courts by way of a defamation action because of the absolute privilege of members of Parliament which applies to things said in the House and in committee. Nor do they have any recourse by way of an application to quash a committee report because the courts have no jurisdiction with regard to the internal proceedings of the House. Finally, the nature of these procedural matters raises a larger question: the relationship of parliamentary committees to courts of law. Should evidence be taken only on sworn testimony, as is the case in courts? Should something designed as an investigation be allowed to change into an adversarial proceeding with a witness being treated like an accused and with a verdict on his behaviour included in a committee report when no charges have even been laid? These questions all involve the status of parliamentary committees and the extent to which their practices should adhere to some of the common procedural safeguards recognized in law.

Instead of summoning witnesses to obtain information, committees frequently request the right to travel. The statistics suggest that there is a trend toward more frequent committee travel in the new system. When committees travel simultaneously, it is difficult to maintain quorum levels in the House and in the remaining committees. However, travelling plays an important part in ensuring that individual members participate in satisfying ways in the legislative process. It may create management problems for the government, but it allows some direct contact between representatives and the represented since parliamentary activities are neither televised nor broadcast.

Committee hearings and travel afford public access to a major institution in the legislative system. Unfortunately, since the committee system acts on policy only after the major commitments and decisions have been taken, the impact of this channel of communication on the formation of public policy is often reduced. In part, this state of affairs springs from the government's concern that active committees may encourage bipartisan positions and even internal party dissent. In this field a new compromise is required: committees should be permitted to take part earlier in the policy-making process in exchange for curtailing their activity in the later stages. Specifically, committees will require a regular flow of general references and annual departmental reports so that they may initiate inquiries into fields *before* the government tables legislation. When bills are tabled, however, committees may be obliged to restrict the kind of investigation and the type of travel they are accustomed to undertake.

c. *Committee Authorities and Support*

Leadership is one of the most important but least understood aspects of committee behaviour. At the commencement of every session the whip arranges for each committee to hold an organizational meeting to elect a chairman. Committee chairmen are therefore technically elected by the committee itself, but the government takes a major hand in deciding which individuals will become chairmen in most committees. In the final analysis, election is the product of a consultative process among the House leaders, the whips, and the ministers involved. This means that in majority situations almost all chairmen are from the government side of the House. In the 28th Parliament an opposition member chaired the Public Accounts Committee, whereas in the 29th Parliament (and a minority government) more chairmen and vice-chairmen were drawn from the opposition.

Like any elected official, the chairman is expected to preside over committee meetings, maintain decorum, and decide questions of order subject to appeal. The standing orders fail to specify the role and functions of committee chairmen beyond these broad notions. Since chairmanships are often considered either stepping stones to greater heights or consolation prizes for those not appointed to the cabinet, there are pressures on the chairman to help the government achieve its legislative and policy goals. At the same time the rules imply that chairmen of committees should be as impartial as the Speaker. Therefore, under present practice chairmen have two somewhat contradictory roles; one as the instrument of the government and another as an impartial official. This difficulty has been compounded by the absence of any institutional arrangement whereby chairmen, House leaders and whips might be drawn together to discuss mutual problems and to schedule committee activities. No effort has been made to correct inconsistencies in the practices and rulings of committee chairmen and little cooperation between the parties can be expected in an atmosphere of controversy over the chairman's proper role. Decisions need to be made about how committee chairmen are supposed to act and how they can best coordinate and supervise committee activity.

Direct government leadership for committees is provided by the responsible cabinet minister and his parliamentary secretary (who is usually a member of the committee). As a general rule ministers are present at the introduction of a bill in committee and frequently when estimates are being discussed. At such times, members feel they are making a useful contribution to the parliamentary system as opposed to merely talking about problems of the day with public servants and other backbenchers. Statistics indicate that on average ministers attended 20 per cent of committee meetings in the second session of the 28th Parliament. They also indicate that parliamentary secretaries attended a much smaller percentage of meetings than other members (62 per cent for the average member compared to 41.1 per cent for the average parliamentary secretary). Prime ministers, however, continue to refuse requests to appear before parliamentary committees.

Since committees are extensions of the House, and not the government, there are no standing orders with respect to the duties of ministers or parliamentary secretaries within committees. Moreover, governments have provided little direction to ministers or parliamentary secretaries about their general role in committees. In the 28th Parliament it was clear that parliamentary secretaries were responsible for government leadership on committees. They were to advocate the government's position on procedural questions, to accompany public service witnesses presenting evidence to committees, and, in the absence of the minister, to set forth government policy and defend it before the committee. Parliamentary secretaries are usually regarded by their colleagues as purely partisan committee members whose task is to defend the government's interest on contentious amendments and to act as a liaison between the committees and caucus. Unfortunately, not all committees have parliamentary secretaries and some committees encompass more than one ministry. When there is no one to do the work of the minister, the chairman is automatically forced to become the arm of the government, thereby compounding the problem of his role in the system.

Committee deliberations are expedited by the efforts of several parliamentary organizations. Continual support is supplied by the Committees and Private Legislation Branch of the House, the Research Branch of the Library of Parliament and the Parliamentary Centre. The Committees Branch provides procedural and administrative support to committees. When the budget of the House of Commons tripled between 1964 and 1972, the Committees Branch accounted for a large proportion of the increase. In 1972 it included eighteen committee clerks plus a chief and deputy chief. Despite its aggrandizement, it has never been staffed with subject-matter specialists and could not readily change its focus from procedural to substantive issues even if a major organizational change was contemplated. Research is provided by the Parliamentary Centre, which aids the Standing Committee on External Affairs and National Defence, and by the staff of the Research Branch of the Library of Parliament which aids all other committees. In 1972 the Research Branch consisted of twenty-two researchers, but most of its research was for individual members, and less than 5 per cent of its time was devoted to committee requests.

Clearly, none of these agencies have the means to supply the research required for all committees in the new, specialized system. Instead, committees tend to rely on ad hoc arrangements which reinforce the difficulty of obtaining a permanent and adequate research organization.

It is likely that the future reform of Parliament will focus on the committee system and the improvement of its support facilities. The committees provide an excellent forum for change because their expressed purpose is to enhance both the effectiveness and efficiency of the House. As the demands for increased committee support are met the bond between committees and the House will have to be adjusted. There are many Canadian parliamentarians on both sides of the House who are prepared to advocate such an evolution. But the aggrandizement of committees means increased pressure on party cohesion. This dilemma will not be resolved until there is agreement on a model for committee activity in the Canadian legislative system in which the realities of party politics are accommodated.

NOTES

1. For comment on the old committee system, see J. R. Mallory, "The Uses of Legislative Committees," *Canadian Public Administration*, Vol. IV, no. 1 (March 1963), pp. 1-14. On the post-1968 system see Hockin, "The Advance of Standing Committees in Canada's House of Commons: 1965-1970," and C. E. S. Franks, "The Dilemma of the Standing Committees of the Canadian House of Commons," *Canadian Journal of Political Science,* Vol. IV, no. 4 (December 1971), pp. 461-476. Specific committee studies include J. R. Mallory and B. A. Smith, "The Legislative Role of Parliamentary Committees in Canada," *Canadian Public Administration*, Vol. XV, no. 1 (March 1972), pp. 1-23, and R. B. Byers, "Perceptions of Parliamentary Surveillance of the Executive," *Canadian Journal of Political Science*, Vol. V, no. 2 (June 1972), pp. 234-250.
2. *Journals*, 3rd Session, 14th Parliament, p. 620.

7. Political Actors in the Legislative System

The institutions described in the preceding chapters form the legislative structure of representative government in Canada. Representative government is supposed to be an institutionalized arrangement whereby the elected are held accountable for their actions by periodic elections and the governors are restrained by the collective vigilance of the elected assembly. Electors are considered to be involved in the legislative system in the sense that members of Parliament represent their views and initiate policy on their behalf. Distinguishing between representative and other forms of government requires, therefore, an assessment of the government's capacity for responsiveness and of the role of representatives in the entire legislative system.

In the Canadian political system there is some doubt about the degree to which representatives are and can be responsive to their electors. Representatives establish relationships with sectors of the political environment other than their own electoral districts. They must reconcile the demands of organized interests, the constraints of party loyalty and the dictates of individual conscience. Even within their own constituencies the scope of representation has increased dramatically. In 1896 each MP represented just over 6,000 voters; by 1974 this had increased to approximately 80,000 for the average member. The lack of voter knowledge on specific political issues prevents politicians from effectively embodying the attitudes and opinions of the electorate. Furthermore, electoral research indicates that the policy positions of individual candidates have little effect on electoral success. Finally, in the Canadian legislative system the opportunity for initiatives by individual members of Parliament is severely restricted by the dominance of the inner circle in all facets of government. It is within these constraints that Canadian legislators must solve the intricate problems of representation.

REPRESENTATIVES AND THE REPRESENTED

Some scholars believe that the puzzle of representation will be solved if the representative assembly mirrors the basic attributes of the population. Proponents of proportional representation, for example, allege that if the social divisions in society are reproduced in Parliament, they will have an impact on the content of legislative output. It is assumed that such representatives will act to defend the interests of their constituents. In Canada it is well known that an accurate resemblance between the representatives and the represented is approximated only in a few select characteristics. Canadian legislators, by and large, constitute an elite which is easily distinguishable from the remainder of the population.

The data available on the attributes of Canadian legislators are fragmentary, but enough individual studies have been completed to suggest a consistent pattern of over- and under-representation. Aggregate data comparisons show that there are marked differences between elected representatives and the general public on the basis of age, education and occupation. MPs have generally been older than their constituents, a fact not particularly surprising since a large proportion of the Canadian population is under 21. According to the 1971 census, 42.2 per cent of Canadians were under the age of 21 while the median age of parliamentarians in the 29th Parliament was 47. The educational status of members is also unrepresentative of the population. The 1961 census indicates that only 6 per cent of Canadians had achieved a college education while 72 per cent of MPs in the 25th Parliament and 67 per cent in the 26th Parliament had been to university.[1] Occupational differences constitute a further division between representatives and the represented. Data from the 25th Parliament show that 51 per cent of Canadian MPs were professionals, 25 per cent proprietor-managers, 12 per cent farmers and 12 per cent low status.[2] Membership in the 26th Parliament reveals similar occupational tendencies. Using the Blishen occupational scale to rank the population Caroline Andrew found that almost 75 per cent of parliamentarians in the 26th Parliament were in the top two groups on the scale, while only 12 per cent of the population (1951 census) were similarly situated.[3] Members with high-status occupations were more likely to belong to the Liberals and Conservatives than either the NDP or the Social Credit party.

With a few important exceptions, differences between representatives and the represented are less pronounced in the areas of religion and ethnicity. In both the 25th and 26th Parliaments British and French descendants were slightly over-represented. Those constituents of other European origins were slightly under-represented, while indigenous Canadians—Eskimos, Indians and Métis—were hardly represented at all. Minority religious affiliations, like minority ethnic groups, also tend to have few members in the House of Commons. On the other hand, an approximate balance has been maintained between the proportion of Catholic representatives and Catholics in the population. Protestant denominations, particularly the United Church of Canada, have been consistently over-represented. Jean Laponce reports that between 1911 and 1953 all Protestant denominations were generally over-represented in the House of Commons but that the proportion of Anglicans decreased dramatically between 1940 and 1953.[4]

If elected representatives comprise an identifiable elite on the basis of the factors discussed above, cabinet ministers constitute an even more select circle. In Canada cabinet ministers are chosen partially on the basis of criteria which give expression to the federal principle. According to this principle every province, where possible, must receive a ministerial appointment and ethnic representation must be delicately balanced. In spite of these apparent constraints on cabinet choice, Canadian prime ministers have managed to appoint individuals with background characteristics which separate them to some extent from other members of Parliament. Cabinet ministers have an overwhelming tendency to be native-born and of British or French descent. Educational standards for cabinet are slightly higher than those for the House. Since 1867 over 80 per cent of cabinet ministers have had some university education and, in 1970, 90 per cent of the Trudeau cabinet were in this category. Lawyers are even more heavily represented among the elected members of the inner circle than they are in the House of Commons. During the period from Confederation to the Second World War, 60 per cent of federal cabinet ministers were trained in the legal profession. These facts indicate that while the House of Commons is not representative of the population, the cabinet is even less so. John Porter has aptly depicted the situation: "The extension of democracy has brought about not a widening, but a further narrowing in the occupational background of the political directorate."[5]

When the ideal of representation is taken to be a direct and accurate reflection of the interests of the represented it is assumed that the personal characteristics of representatives will ensure that they act to defend the interests they mirror. Studies of all Canadian members of Parliament have revealed that distortions exist between representatives and the represented, especially in age, sex, education, and occupational patterns. A perfect reproduction of basic societal attributes in a legislature is probably impossible and discrepancies of this kind exist in all developed democracies. However, no one in Canada has demonstrated that differences between representatives and the represented have an impact on actual behaviour or on public policy. Before evaluations may be made as to whether the public interest is affected by the personal background characteristics of MPs one must examine actual legislative behaviour. Numerous, even conflicting, environmental factors exert pressure on MPs to act in particular ways and this necessarily compromises the mirror-image notion of representation. The actual behaviour of members of Parliament adds a new dimension to the concept of representation.

LEGISLATIVE BEHAVIOUR: THE OUTSIDE AND INSIDE MODELS

Both "inside" and "outside" models are employed to describe and explain the overt actions of legislators. Those institutional arrangements, patterns of influence, and norms of behaviour whose source is within the institutional boundaries of the legislature are the cluster of "inside" variables. The caucus would, for example, count as an "inside" variable. Those factors which influence parliamentarians' attitudes toward behaviour prior to their election to Parliament and those factors which have a continual influence on behaviour from beyond the institutional boundary of the legislature (such as interest groups) are the cluster of "outside" variables. The working hypothesis underlying most of the research on legislative behaviour is that these variables can be used to explain why legislators choose one course of action over another.

Of primary importance for the hypothesis that the behaviour of MPs may be explained by the outside model are the social background variables discussed above. It is often assumed that a group of individuals who share characteristics such as educational achievement or occupational background are likely to behave in the same way. French-Canadian MPs, for example, are expected to defend government attempts to promote the use of the French language outside Quebec. Regardless of how illuminating this idea may seem for an understanding of behaviour, the personal attributes of MPs are often unreliable predictors. For example, while no efforts have been made to study their behaviour in the Canadian Parliament, it has been shown that lawyers in the American Congress and state legislatures do not vote as a bloc and, therefore, this aspect of their behaviour may not be predicted by their occupational backgrounds.[6]

The socialization and recruitment patterns of Canadian legislators may also be considered outside variables. Socialization refers to the process of learning political attitudes and skills; recruitment concerns the process through which the anticipated rewards of legislative participation are communicated to a prospective participant. The tendency among social scientists has been to treat these factors as dependent variables. Thus, Allan Kornberg discovered a strong correlation between the time of political socialization of MPs and the agents which performed the socialization function.[7] David Hoffman and Norman Ward found a low level of self-recruitment and a high incidence of party involvement in the recruitment process.[8] Unfortunately, neither of these findings were then correlated with subsequent behaviour in the House of Commons. The findings provide descriptive information about Canadian legislators but no indication of the significance of this information for legislative behaviour.

It seems reasonable to assume that an individual's style of behaviour and his parliamentary goals will be affected by his previous political experiences. However, many legislators in Canada are without the advantage, or the disadvantage, of exposure to partisan politics. While once a common attribute of federal politicians, one-quarter to one-third of MPs in recent Parliaments have had no prior political experience, even at the level of office-holding within the party. The New Democrats were the most experienced MPs in the 25th and 26th Parliaments while the Liberals had the least prior experience in the earlier Parliament and Social Credit and Créditiste MPs in the later Parliament.[9] Among those few members who have had prior political experience most have obtained it in a party organization. In an indirect attempt to relate these previous experiences and the background characteristics of MPs to legislative behaviour, Kornberg examined the hypothesis that these factors have an impact on the formation of parliamentarians' goals. He found, for example, that the better educated the MP, the more likely he was to adopt as a personal goal the initiation or evaluation of public policy. However, other background variables and the prior political experiences of legislators proved weak indicators of their propensity to choose particular legislative goals.[10]

One might expect that the type of constituency a member represents would influence the judgments he is required to make in the legislature. American research has demonstrated that a candidate's district, its geographic location or its economic base, has an influence on roll-call voting in Congress. This is not surprising in an undisciplined party system where representatives must weigh heavily factors other than their party affiliation. However, little information exists to demonstrate a connection between constituency characteristics and the behaviour of Canadian members of Parliament. There is some evidence to the contrary. Lovink advises that in the opinion of members of the 28th Parliament the level of competitiveness in a constituency was an inconsequential factor in the allocation of political benefits.[11] Of course, the degree of constituency competitiveness does affect the nature of representative government. In Canada, where the level of electoral competition is extraordinarily high, the level of political experience is correspondingly low with the result that legislative institutions are frequently staffed by novices.

In addition to employing constituency differences to account for legislative behaviour, it is possible to define an MP's behaviour in terms of his constituency activity *per se*. Hoffman and Ward examined the links MPs establish with their constituents and suggested how outside variables may be used to account for differences in an MP's style of constituency politics. Political information was found to be received in different ways and from numerous sources: 58 per cent of respondents mentioned conversations with constituents, 35 per cent mentioned conversations with party organizers and only a few cited letters (8 per cent) or opinion polls (6 per cent). Hoffman and Ward also discovered that MPs from rural areas were more inclined to rely on personal conversations as a source of information and less inclined to rely on the party than urban members. However, the authors were unable to use the variables of language, party, and region to predict the manner in which MPs are informed by their constituents. On the other hand, when it came to communicating information to constituents, regional factors did have an impact on members' style. MPs from Atlantic and western provinces were more inclined than others to spend shorter periods of time in their constituencies. Language also emerged as an important variable. Not only were French-speaking members more inclined to maintain a constituency office, but they also spent more time in their constituencies and were less likely to move their families to Ottawa.[12]

When an individual is elected to Parliament he is inducted into its norms and standards of behaviour. Like all freshmen he is influenced by the formal structures as well as the informal patterns of influence. Many of these inside variables were alluded to in the earlier treatment of parliamentary and preparliamentary structures and suggestions were made regarding their impact on legislative behaviour. On the floor of the House formal rules limit the length of speeches and demand that their contents be relevant to the discussion at hand. In committees the rule which permits frequent membership changes impedes the development of individual expertise and committee autonomy. In other words, the formal requirements in a legislative system set the parameters of legislative behaviour and frequently become the source of informal patterns of influence.

Norms or folkways or rules of the game help sustain the continuity of the legislature and ensure that individual legislators are aware of what other MPs consider requirements for effective action. Norms exist in all groups and the nature of the situation determines the norm in effect. According to those who rely on the inside model, these unwritten rules can be accurate predictors of legislative behaviour. However, a system of norms may be more or less accepted, and in any particular case competing norms may apply. The heavy turnover in Canadian legislative membership undermines the continuity of the learning process and keeps the behavioural standards in a state of flux. In such circumstances it is to be expected that parties, which are part of both the inside and outside models, will be the main agents in the socialization process.

Substructures in Parliament offer perhaps the best opportunity for studying the impact of norms on individual behaviour. Small groups, such as committees, allow frequent and close interaction and the occasional relaxation of party discipline. The norms which develop may influence the level of partisanship in different committee proceedings. When committees undertake general investigations partisanship is often less pronounced than in the consideration of legislation. Furthermore, most committees will not convene a meeting unless a member of the opposition is present, while some will not proceed in the examination of witnesses unless this condition is fulfilled. Some committees have minimum levels of attendance for hearing witnesses, others do not. None of these rules are specified by the standing orders but they are recognized as established customs in particular committees. More stringent rules govern the behaviour of government backbenchers. Parliamentary secretaries, for example, act as the source of informal cues regarding speeches, questions, and ultimately votes in committees.

In his research on the Canadian House of Commons

Kornberg has emphasized the significance of established conventions.[13] Among those norms cited by MPs in the 25th Parliament were requirements to minimize personal conflict, avoid conduct which reflects poorly on Parliament, reinforce existing party divisions, and establish expertise in some subject matter, Kornberg found that the length of legislative service had a minor impact on the ability to articulate these norms. It appears that informal rules of this type are an intrinsic part of most social situations and freshmen MPs are neither ignorant nor bewildered when they first encounter them in the legislative system. New Democrats tended to be more aware than others of norms within the House, while MPs with a college education and those who did not consider themselves in conflict with either party or constituency were among those most aware of norms outside the House. Of course, errors may be committed by even the most highly placed parliamentarians. In the 28th Parliament Prime Minister Trudeau stumbled into the gravest type when he suggested that once MPs were off Parliament Hill, they were "nobodies."

While members of Parliament were able to cite a wide variety of norms, 83.6 per cent claimed to be unaware of any sanctions that could be applied inside the House, and 47.5 per cent claimed to be unaware of sanctions outside the House. Kornberg suggests that the sanction system may not be working properly because of a lack of consensus on the MP's place in the legislative system. It is true that a lack of agreement exists about the role of the member of Parliament, but party norms continue to foster cohesion in Canadian parliamentary parties. Since Canadian MPs, like their British counterparts, only conceive of politics in terms of parties, they are probably sceptical of the idea that sanctions can be used to manufacture party loyalty. The notion of party is imbedded so deeply in the perceptions of Canadian parliamentarians that little consideration is given to the consequences of independent action.

Paradoxically, the investigation of legislative customs may be impeded by the fact that norms exist with regard to answering questions about norms. Members may feel they are required to emphasize collegiality, withhold "trade secrets," appear conversant with the rules, and cite standing orders. Some MPs are unwilling to express their personal views and simply ask their assistants to fill in questionnaires for them. In view of these facts, consideration has even been given to screening social science research on the Hill to prevent what some parliamentarians call a distorted image of Parliament.

The most salient inside variable, and indeed the most important variable of all in a parliamentary system, is party affiliation.[14] Cohesive political parties, as we have emphasized, are essential to the operation of the legislative system and individual behaviour cannot be assessed without a consideration of this variable. This is especially the case with respect to a particular aspect of behaviour in the House—voting. In the American Congress and in the state legislatures party affiliation is by no means a reliable predictor of voting behaviour. In Canada, on the other hand, its predictive capacity outweighs that of all the other inside and outside variables put together. Except for the odd free vote, an individual's vote almost always indicates a personal commitment to the parliamentary party, not to one or another side of a political issue.

In the Canadian parliamentary system there are few indicators of individual behaviour whose meaning is undisputed.[15] To get behind the division lists and examine aspects of behaviour other than party voting is a formidable task and one that does not yield easily to the collection of data. To accept "inside" views of caucus deliberation is clearly unsatisfactory. There are, of course, public activities a member may undertake in his constituency, as we have mentioned earlier, and his behaviour in committees and in parliamentary debates may be examined. But in each case researchers must develop valid indicators of the concept they are considering. If they are examining the sources of rebellious or parochial behaviour, convincing arguments must be made that the activities they are studying represent valid examples. Few Canadian political scientists have attempted this type of research.

LEGISLATIVE BEHAVIOUR: ROLE THEORY

Many social scientists have suggested that the concept of "role" may provide a means of explaining legislative behaviour.

The term refers to the expectations associated with a particular position in a social system and individuals usually hold many roles. Political roles are fashioned by two forces; first, the individual's own perceptions and expectations of the formal position and, second, the perceptions and expectations of others in related positions. The analysis of legislative roles changes the research emphasis from the actual behaviour of MPs to their personal attitudes and from particular actions to general dispositions. Role is an attractive concept primarily because it effectively summarizes all of the attitudes that are likely to be evoked in any particular circumstance. It is a means of encompassing the entire legislature at the individual level of analysis and it emphasizes that behaviour always takes place in an atmosphere of expectations.

Legislators usually agree on the general norms that govern behaviour in a legislative system, but often find it necessary to choose from among divergent norms in particular circumstances. Competing norms give rise to competing role orientations. Canadian MPs disagree on the types of relationships they should establish with their clientele, party, and the citizens they represent. For our purposes representational roles are the most illuminating. In their research on American legislators Eulau and his colleagues offered a threefold classification of representational roles: the trustee, the delegate, and the politico.[16] Representatives who adopt the trustee role consider themselves free agents who act on their own judgment after appraising each situation. The delegate, on the other hand, feels at least partially committed to follow the instructions of his constituents. For some this simply means consultation and possibly some type of constraint, but it may also be considered a mandatory instruction. The politico is a mixture of these pure types. A legislator who is a politico may assume the roles serially (first the trustee then the delegate role) or he may attempt to reconcile them in which case he is made particularly sensitive to role conflict. Canadian students of role orientations have made some adjustments to these concepts. Kornberg refers to delegates as delegate-servants, and Hoffman and Ward introduce the term "party delegate" to refer to those who receive instructions from the party and the term "constituency delegate" to refer to those instructed by their constituents.[17]

Kornberg found that of the legislators interviewed in his study of the 25th Parliament, 15 per cent were trustees, 36 per cent were politicos, and 49 per cent were delegate-servants.[18] In the 26th Parliament Hoffman and Ward uncovered a greater number of trustees (33 per cent), but precisely the same proportion of politicos. Of the remaining delegates 18 per cent were party delegates and 12 per cent were constituency delegates.[19] While some discrepancy exists in these figures they demonstrate that Canadian MPs are inclined to accept some type of instruction. When stimulated by party loyalty this type of compliance is highly functional to cohesive parties and consequently to a British parliamentary form of government.

Role orientation is usually considered a product of the same variables discussed with the inside and outside models of legislative behaviour. At the level of the political system it may be presumed that the political culture has an initial and lasting impact on the selection of role orientations because it is the culture which effectively structures the MPs' alternatives. Selected correlations from the major studies illustrate the possible sources of particular role orientations in the Canadian context. Kornberg found that education and occupation were related to the propensity to choose one role orientation over another. Those who were college graduates, businessmen and professionals tended to assume the trustee role more frequently.[20] In the Hoffman and Ward study MPs with a background in municipal politics were slightly more inclined to a constituent-delegate role, MPs over 60 years of age tended toward a party-delegate orientation, and those with little prior political experience were inclined to adopt a trustee role.[21] When the MP perceived his constituency as competitive Kornberg also found an inclination to adopt a delegate-servant role.[22] Among the inside variables party affiliation once again proved to be significant. Kornberg showed that members of "left-wing" parties (Liberals and NDP) were more inclined to be trustees while Hoffman and Ward found this tendency to be strongest among the NDP.

Knowledge of a legislator's role orientation would be an additional advantage in predicting his behaviour, but scholars have experienced difficulty establishing relationships between these two variables. In the first place the strength with which roles are held may affect attempts at role enactment. Some individuals hold a particular role with great determination while others give it little consideration. Legislators may also find that the decisions they are called upon to make are so complicated that their personal role orientation is of little help in directing their behaviour. Or, they may change their attitude when confronted with an actual policy choice. Most important, while members hold particular role orientations they rarely arrive at personal judgments which differ from those of their party. Kornberg found that only 25 per cent of MPs interviewed considered a caucus decision always binding,[23] and only 57 per cent of MPs in the Hoffman and Ward study claimed they would abide by the party in the case of a conflict with their personal views.[24] It is curious, however, that division lists do not reflect such independent behaviour! In all of these cases the relevance of a classification of roles for predicting behaviour in the Canadian setting is suspect. Regardless of the role MPs claim to adopt, for the purposes of role enactment when voting on the floor of the House all are party delegates.

OPPORTUNITIES FOR INITIATIVE: PRIVATE MEMBERS' BILLS

The distribution of role orientations among Canadian MPs may be considered a distribution of their personal sentiments. In affirming particular role orientations legislators are at least expressing their aspirations. The most general aspirations expressed can be considered purposive roles—MPs' attitudes about what they hope to accomplish in their position. In the Kornberg study 47 per cent of the legislators had a policy or law-making orientation, 23 per cent were constituency oriented, while 30 per cent combined the two orientations in some manner.[25] Hoffman and Ward found that nearly 80 per cent of their respondents characterized their position at least partially as "liaison officer" (links between constituents and the national government) and that 51 per cent of English-speaking respondents and 65 per cent of French-speaking respondents mentioned a "law-maker" task.[26] Both studies remarked on the apparent incongruity involved in accepting a law-maker orientation in a system where the scope for individual policy initiation is extraordinarily limited. An opportunity to satisfy this particular orientation is afforded by the private members' bill, but for several reasons it is an unsatisfactory vehicle.

Considerable parliamentary time is made available for non-government initiated activity. Each session furnishes forty periods of one hour on Mondays and Tuesdays and an unspecified number of such periods on Thursdays and Fridays for the consideration of private members' business. But the usual 5 p.m. to 6 p.m. time period is not conducive to public or even parliamentary attention. And when private members' business is called by the Chair, not all of it centres on private members' bills. In March of 1972, for example, six of the eight hours on private members' business were devoted to motions. For the private member the notice of motion is an attractive means of advocating general plans of action or moral positions. Unlike the private members' bill it avoids the necessity for legal jargon and is considered a device which expresses sentiments without being encumbered by legal, and sometimes practical, considerations. Moreover, it is usually possible to construct such motions without contradicting party policy.

A private members' bill is a public bill which is sponsored by a private member, does not form part of the government's legislative program and, theoretically, does not require the allocation of public funds. It is one of the few occasions in which the pre-parliamentary stages of the legislative system are not involved in the ultimate parliamentary process. No effort has been made by students of Parliament to correlate the tendency to cite a law-maker orientation with the inclination to introduce private members' bills. However, some indication of a relationship is provided by the fact that members of the NDP are by far the most inclined to use this vehicle. It is not unusual to find that, proportionately, they sponsor ten or even twenty times the number introduced by members of other parties. New Democrats are also more likely than members of other parties to hold a trustee role orientation and to consider law-making a primary goal.[27]

Not all "law-makers" can be expected to use private members' bills as a means of fulfilling their parliamentary goals. In the first place, very few private members' bills are ever passed. Secondly, those few bills which do not meet parliamentary approval are often concerned with innocuous topics, particularly the renaming of electoral districts. Those that succeed are usually passed on the strength of the government's majority. Most of these bills, however, are not even discussed on the floor of the House. In the 28th Parliament over 80 per cent of private members' bills never reached the second reading stage and approximately 10 per cent of those that did were "talked out" in the allotted hour and had to be dropped to the bottom of the order paper, from which they never reemerged. Those bills which met with success included such proposals as the prevention of the use of the term "Parliament Hill" for commercial purposes and the adoption of a national "Pollution Week."

Despite the dismal fate that awaits most private members' bills, parliamentarians continue to introduce them in ever greater quantities. In the 24th Parliament an average of 46 private members' bills were introduced per session, but by the 26th Parliament this had increased to 102, and by the 28th Parliament it was an average of 195 per session.[28] Those MPs who introduce this type of legislation seem content to offer a concrete expression of opinion and seldom aspire to have the bills they bring before the House enacted. On occasion the subject-matter obtains consideration in a standing committee even when the bill is not acceptable. An example was the private member's bill which proposed the elimination of advertisements on children's television programs. Simply making their views public is often sufficient incentive for most members, although some undoubtedly use these bills to demonstrate their diligence to constituents.

The main difficulty in satisfying a law-maker orientation with this instrument is the lack of government feedback. Members may believe they influence government policy in this manner and there is no justification for denying the possibility.

However, the government seldom credits private members' bills with any policy influence. From the government's point of view, their own backbenchers can use caucus to influence pending policy. Opposition MPs, on the other hand, are not considered to be involved in government policy-making. Thus in addition to technical and administrative difficulties there are political dilemmas involved in openly entertaining the ideas contained in private members' bills.

Beyond the cabinet's unreceptive attitude toward private members' bills there are two other problems. First, it is by no means certain that government departments are aware of, or react to, these initiatives. No format for departmental replies is in use and the decision to react to such bills is left to the discretion of individual departments. Secondly, although very few private members' bills are considered worthwhile by departments, MPs are seldom, if ever, informed of the difficulties with their suggestions. A glaring general deficiency in many of the private members' bills is legislative drafting. This factor alone prevents departments from giving some of these bills serious consideration. Nevertheless, some initiatives have been considered potentially useful additions to departmental policy but no effort has been made to acknowledge backbench initiative. The government ought to develop an apparatus to evaluate private members' bills systematically and to communicate their conclusions to Parliament as a whole. Efforts should be made to create a forum where parliamentarians and bureaucrats can discuss MPs' ideas.

It is doubtful that norms or roles are so thoroughly ossified in the Canadian legislative system that new perceptions of the member of Parliament could not be encouraged. In this chapter we have stressed the barriers to role enactment, but there remain opportunities to create legislative institutions which give expression to the personal initiatives of members.

NOTES

1. Allan Kornberg, *Canadian Legislative Behaviour* (Toronto: Holt, Rinehart and Winston, 1967), p. 45; Caroline Andrew, "The Political Background of Members of the Twenty-Sixth House of Commons," (Unpublished thesis, UBC, 1964), p. 27.

2. Kornberg, *op. cit.*, p. 45.
3. Andrew, "Political Background of Members," p. 18.
4. J. A. Laponce, "The Religious Background of Canadian MPs," *Political Studies*, Vol. 6 (1958), pp. 253-258.
5. John Porter, *The Vertical Mosaic* (Toronto: University of Toronto Press, 1965), p. 392.
6. A discussion of the inside and outside model and research in the American context can be found in Heinz Eulau and Katherine Hinckley, "Legislative Institutions and Processes," in James A. Robinson, ed., *Political Science Annual 1966* (New York: Bobbs-Merrill Co., 1966), pp. 85-190.
7. Kornberg, *op. cit.,* p. 50.
8. David Hoffman and Norman Ward, *Bilingualism and Biculturalism in the Canadian House of Commons*; Document No. 3 of the Royal Commission on Bilingualism and Biculturalism (Ottawa: Queen's Printer, 1970), pp. 61-63.
9. Kornberg, *op. cit.*, p. 54; Hoffman and Ward, *op. cit.*, p. 64.
10. Kornberg, *op. cit.*, p. 90.
11. J. A. A. Lovink, "Is Canadian Politics too Competitive?" *Canadian Journal of Political Science,* Vol. VI (December 1973), p. 372.
12. Hoffman and Ward, *op. cit.*, Chapter V.
13. Allan Kornberg, "Rules of the Game in the Canadian House of Commons," *Journal of Politics,* Vol 26 (1964), pp. 358-80.
14. Many other inside variables could be mentioned but there has been little research on their effect on behaviour. The amount of professional support staff, for example, is a factor which may eventually effect legislative norms and the opinion MPs have of themselves in the legislative system.
15. In the United Kingdom the existence of procedural devices, such as Early Day Motions, and party factions which organize propaganda campaigns provide opportunities which do not exist in Canada to examine backbench opinion. See S. E. Finer, H. B. Berrington, and D. J. Bartholomew, *Backbench Opinion in the House of Commons 1955-59* (Oxford: Pergamon Press, 1961); Robert J. Jackson, *Rebels and Whips* (London: Macmillan, 1968).
16. H. Eulau, "The Legislator as Representative: Representational Roles," in John Wahlke, *et al., The Legislative System,* (New York: John Wiley and Sons, 1962), pp. 267-286.
17. It has been pointed out that the representational role a member chooses is not the same as his areal focus. For example, not all trustees believe they represent the entire nation. Canadian political scientists have stressed this distinction.
18. Kornberg, *Canadian Legislative Behaviour*, pp. 106-108.
19. Hoffman and Ward, *op. cit.*, pp. 66-77.

20. Kornberg, *op. cit.*, p. 109.
21. Hoffman and Ward, *op. cit.*, pp. 70-72.
22. Kornberg, *op. cit.*, p. 109.
23. Kornberg, *op. cit.*, p. 131.
24. Hoffman and Ward, *op. cit.*, p. 74.
25. Kornberg, *op. cit.*, pp. 79-83.
26. Hoffman and Ward, *op. cit.*, pp. 83-86.
27. The latter finding is from Allan Kornberg, "Some Differences in Role Perceptions Among Canadian Legislators." (unpublished Ph.D. thesis University of Michigan, 1964), but Hoffman and Ward detected no significant relationship between party affiliation and purposive role orientations, p. 84.
28. Stewart Hyson, "The Role of the Backbencher: An Analysis of Private Members' Bills in the Canadian House of Commons," unpublished paper, December 1973.

8. Problems and Prospects in Evaluating Legislative Activity and Reform

The evaluation of political institutions has been a traditional and fundamental part of political philosophy. Based on assumptions about the nature of man and the political community, students of politics have continuously offered prescriptions for more suitable political organization. However, in the 1950s and 1960s, as more scholars began to lend their support to the idea of a "science" of politics, there developed a marked tendency to avoid political evaluation. Indeed, many empirically oriented political scientists claimed that the evaluation of policies or institutions lay outside the ambit of a value-free social science. Evaluations require standards of value, and the establishment of such standards is a subjective exercise, unamenable to scientific procedures or arbitration. Clearly this type of attitude has had some positive ramifications for the discipline of political science but it has also meant that the tools of social science have been applied only randomly to the evaluation of political structures and public policies. A complementary attitude exists among some members of Parliament. It is not uncommon to hear espoused the view that the very nature of legislative institutions disqualifies them from evaluation by social scientists. The predominance of competing ideologies and personalities, it is argued, makes political, not rational, discourse the order of the day.

The attitudes of political scientists and politicians seem to be changing. In recent years the absence of explicit and systematic evaluations of political systems has been condemmed by political scientists,[1] and in Canada, more academics have been employed in the development of ideas and judgments about political institutions. In fact, the data assembled by social scientists are now considered an absolute necessity for the task of evaluation.

There are basic problems in the application of social science to the reform of political institutions. While there is general agreement that evaluation involves the measurement of success in achieving a stated purpose or objective,[2] it is practically impossible to secure agreement on the purposes of legislatures. In the United States it has been pointed out that "the evaluation of Congressional performance has been fragmentary and disappointing"[3] and "the reformers' premises concerning the proper functions of Congress remain unarticulated or indistinct, or even contradictory."[4] In Canada lack of agreement on the purpose of Parliament has been compounded by the fusion of the executive and legislative branches of government.[5] It is unclear whether Parliament is supposed to emphasize the refining of legislation, for example, or the surveillance of the executive. In Chapter 2 we listed several functions that the legislative system may be expected to perform. However, we are forced to limit our approach in this chapter because, at present, there are few functions amenable to systematic evaluative research. Ultimately, of course, all evaluations of legislative performance will depend on value judgments about the purposes of legislatures.

In theory, the methodology of evaluative research is the same as non-evaluative research. As Edward Suchman puts it, "ultimately the significance of the results will be determined according to the same scientific standards. . . ."[6] Science requires the formulation and testing of hypothesis and this usually entails some element of quantification. For some the prospect of quantifying legislative activities is an anathema. Even advocates of more systematic evaluation have emphasized that the language of value is full of metaphors and allusions. Robert Dahl has pointed out that, "to those who love the language of value, operational measures rob their poetry of all its beauty, most of its subtlety, and a great deal of its meaning."[7] Eventually, however, evaluations will have to be made using quantitative techniques that permit comparison and scientific generalization. At present even tentative statements based on quantitative studies will complement the impressionistic approach upon which students of the Canadian legislative system often rely.

This chapter examines one function of the legislative system —law-making. While it would be advantageous to include a statistical analysis of the institutions of the inner circle, this is impractical. Measures are difficult to construct for any part of the legislative system, but as the House of Commons conducts its business as a public forum, it is the most attractive focus for preliminary examination. Moreover, some reforms of Parliament have been directed at improving the efficiency of law-making. The relation between reform proposals and their consequences is also an aspect of evaluative research and the latter part of the chapter is devoted to an examination of the impact of the 1968 procedural reforms on law-making in Parliament.

LAW-MAKING IN THE LEGISLATIVE SYSTEM

The data that follow are designed to give a quantitative picture of how Parliament has been performing the law-making function. The performance of legislative decision-making will be expressed as the ratio of time to volume of legislative output. Time, in this sense, is assumed to represent an important resource for both parts of the legislative system: the government and the legislature. The idea of using time as an indicator of cost presumes there is a shortage of it. It must be possible for the legislature to use it more efficiently, which means the source of input cannot periodically dry up while the legislature is ostensibly performing this function. The fact that most conventional procedural weapons, regardless of who employs them, are directed at the time resource is an important indication that time does qualify as an indicator of cost even in parliamentarians' evaluations of legislative decision-making.

The choice of indicators brings some of the problems of evaluative research into sharp relief. First, indicators that emphasize the volume and speed of law-making do not exhaust all that the concept of law-making implies. Abraham Kaplan[8] recounts the story of one of the subjects of Kinsey's study of sexual behaviour who complained, "No matter what I told him he just looked me straight in the eye and asked 'how many times?'." In this case the subject felt that the significance of his activity did not depend on its frequency. Clearly, the question of quality as well as quantity is important in assessing some activities. Unfortunately, it is difficult to develop a consistent, meaningful classification of legislation and almost impossible to achieve agreement on criteria suitable to measure the quality of legislation. Also, judgments based on the content or quality of decisions are often evaluations of governmental and not legislative decision-making.

The second problem comes in evaluating particular levels of legislative output. The reader will have to decide what is the "best" level of legislative output and whether he prefers a slow, methodical (and sometimes obstructive) legislature or one that is responsive (and sometimes over-indulgent). If efficiency is the only value involved, then the more output produced in the same time the better the performance of the law-making function. But rapidity is not the only consideration in law-making and there are functions other than law-making that must also be performed. For example, Parliament must take enough time to debate and consider legislation in order to perform a legitimation function. And if Parliament is slow in law-making the government may attempt to withdraw some of the opportunities available to perform other functions that compete for parliamentary time. It is these considerations that should give pause to the eager evaluator, especially when he considers that a very high level of performance in one activity may be ultimately dysfunctional for the performance of others.

To evaluate the law-making of the House of Commons we have reviewed studies on Parliament since Confederation and analysed in more detail our own data on parliamentary decision-making from 1945 to 1972. Allan Kornberg's research demonstrates clearly that Parliament has been working longer to achieve less in the twentieth than in the nineteenth century. Table 3 shows that the lengths of Parliaments and the number of sitting days have both increased while the percentage of bills introduced and passed has declined. The average number

Table 3: LEGISLATIVE ACTIVITY IN THE CANADIAN HOUSE OF COMMONS, 1867–1968

Parliament	Duration	Type of government	Number of days in session	Number of actual sitting days	Number of bills introduced into parliament	Number of bills passed by parliament	Relative length of parliament (ratio of sitting days to days in session)	Relative success of parliament (ratio of bills passed to bills introduced)	Relative legislative load (bills introduced per day)	Relative legislative output (bills passed per day)
1st	Nov., 1867– June, 1872	Majority	446	283	610	422	.63	.69	2.16	1.49
2nd	Mar., 1873– Nov., 1873	Majority	177	70	157	125	.40	.80	2.24	1.79
3rd	Mar., 1874– May, 1878	Majority	362	262	579	421	.72	.73	2.21	1.61
4th	Feb., 1879– May, 1882	Majority	379	259	523	344	.68	.66	2.02	1.33
5th	Feb., 1883– June, 1886	Majority	472	324	613	406	.69	.66	1.89	1.25
6th	Apr., 1887– May, 1890	Majority	375	256	622	447	.68	.72	2.43	1.75
7th	Apr., 1891– Apr., 1896	Majority	695	458	825	575	.66	.70	1.80	1.26
8th	Aug., 1896– July, 1900	Majority	593	402	739	487	.68	.66	1.84	1.21
9th	Dec., 1900– Sept., 1904	Majority	578	394	748	564	.68	.75	1.90	1.43

10th	Dec., 1904–Sept., 1908	Majority	712	460	786	639	.65	.81	1.71	1.39
11th	Dec., 1908–July, 1911	Majority	491	303	596	423	.62	.71	1.97	1.40
12th	Oct., 1911–Oct., 1917	Majority	870	568	895	726	.65	.81	1.58	1.28
13th	Mar., 1918–Oct., 1921	Union (coalition)	515	355	500	406	.69	.81	1.41	.48
14th	Mar., 1922–Sept., 1925	Minority	549	366	471	370	.67	.78	1.41	1.14
15th	Jan., 1926–July, 1926	Minority	177	111	110	24	.63	.22	.99	.22
16th	Dec., 1926–May, 1930	Majority	439	292	491	396	.66	.81	1.68	1.35
17th	Sept., 1930–Aug., 1935	Majority	772	507	454	359	.66	.79	.89	.71
18th	Feb., 1936–Jan., 1940	Majority	533	365	340	252	.68	.74	.67	.50
19th	May, 1940–Apr., 1945	Majority	1750	565	282	196	.32	.69	.50	.35
20th	Sept., 1945–Apr., 1949	Majority	748	487	439	366	.65	.90	.90	.75
21st	Sept., 1949–June, 1953	Majority	1154	527	473	389	.46	.82	.90	.74
22nd	Nov., 1953–Apr., 1957	Majority	787	507	388	296	.64	.76	.76	.58

Parliament	Duration	Type of government	Number of days in session	Number of actual sitting days	Number of bills introduced into parliament	Number of bills passed by parliament	Relative length of parliament (ratio of sitting days to days in session)	Relative success of parliament (ratio of bills passed to bills introduced)	Relative legislative load (bills introduced per day)	Relative legislative output (bills passed per day)
23rd	Oct., 1957– Feb., 1958	Minority	111	78	62	41	.70	.66	.79	.52
24th	May, 1958– Apr., 1962	Majority	919	605	576	331	.66	.57	.95	.55
25th	Sept., 1962– Feb., 1963	Minority	132	72	127	24	.54	.14	1.76	.33
26th	May, 1963– Sept., 1965	Minority	717	418	528	183	.58	.35	1.26	.44
27th	Jan., 1966– Apr., 1968	Minority	718	405	565	170	.56	.30	1.40	.42

SOURCE: Allan Kornberg, "Parliament in Canadian Society," Allan Kornberg and Lloyd D. Musolf, (eds.), *Legislatures in Developmental Perspective* (Durham, N.C., 1970), pp. 107-108. Reprinted by permission of Duke University Press.

of bills passed per day between the first and eighth Parliaments was 1.39, but between the 19th and 27th Parliaments, the performance ratio fell to .54. However, as Kornberg has observed, the comparability of his data is suspect because the number of private and private members' bills was considerably greater in the nineteenth than in the twentieth century. Furthermore, the modern period is characterized by a government program in which legislation is longer and more complex than it was in earlier periods. Nevertheless, the fact that it now takes longer to pass legislation is an interesting comment on the argument often repeated in the scholarly literature that the government has manipulated parliamentary procedures to make the House of Commons a legislation factory.

In order to evaluate the modern Parliament, postwar data has been assessed in more detail. The changes wrought by the Second World War and the continued development of the positive state make these data more compelling and predictive of future trends than less exhaustive treatments of earlier years. We have also extended the analysis to estimates and miscellaneous matters and have indicated the relations between committee and House performance on all of these subjects.

The legislative performance ratio is the relation between pages of legislative output and the time consumed measured in days of legislative deliberation.[9]

Analysing this ratio session by session produces a rather bumpy line from 1945 to 1972. The right-hand column of Table 4, however, represents a trend line of legislative performance based on a moving average with consecutive groups of four sessions averaged together.[10] With the exception of the first group of four sessions, the trend line produced in Table 4 indicates a steadily declining performance ratio from a high of 5.7 in the sessions between 1948 and 1950 to a low of 2.6 between 1960 and 1963. The sessions between 1964 and 1968 produced a rise in the performance ratio to 3.5 and the next period, 1968 to 1972, reveals a further increase. Table 4 also indicates that during these later periods it required more time to pass an average bill than it had since the end of the war.

The gentle downward trend in performance since Confederation and especially since the war suggests a process of grad-

Table 4: THE LAW-MAKING PERFORMANCE OF THE CANADIAN HOUSE OF COMMONS, SESSION BY SESSION, 1945-1972

Years of four session intervals	Average no. of sitting days	Average no. of public bills enacted	Average no. of days to pass a bill	Number of pages of enacted legislation	Average no. of pages passed per sitting day
1945–47	82.0	40.0	1.7	355.8	4.3
1948–50	83.0	49.0	1.7	473.5	5.7
1951–52	89.0	51.8	1.7	424.8	4.7
1953–57	125.5	54.0	2.3	468.0	3.7
1957–60	111.0	44.3	2.5	381.8	3.4
1960–63	107.0	38.0	2.8	279.0	2.6
1964–68	176.6	52.5	3.4	613.5	3.5
1968–72	171.3	54.3	3.2	629.0	3.7

SOURCE: *Debates of the House of Commons; Statutes of Canada.*

ual atrophy in parliamentary institutions. When environmental changes make existing organizational procedures unsatisfactory, March and Simon hypothesize that the rate of innovation will increase.[11] During the period between 1960 and 1963 when performance ratios were lowest on average, agitation did begin for a review of existing parliamentary procedures. And in 1965 a special committee was appointed to study procedure and organization. Dissatisfaction with organizational structures during this time indicates that at least some members perceived the legislature as having a low level of decision-making performance and that reforms were required.

One of the most fiercely debated explanations of trends in law-making performance is the presence or absence of minority governments. According to some politicians minority governments result in a slow movement of legislation through the House and hence a low performance ratio. Some indication of support for this hypothesis is provided in Table 4. The two periods with the lowest performance ratios together contain six of the seven minority government sessions in the postwar

Table 5: COMPARISON OF LAW-MAKING PERFORMANCE IN MINORITY AND MAJORITY GOVERNMENT SITUATIONS, BY SESSION, 1945–1972

	Number of sessions	Average no. of sitting days	Average no. of public bills enacted	Average no. of days to pass a bill	Average no. of pages of enacted legislation	Average no. of pages passed per sitting day
Minority governments	7	135.3	42.7	3.1	441.3	3.3
Majority governments	25	112.3	50.9	2.2	456.5	4.1

SOURCE: *Debates of the House of Commons; Statutes of Canada.*

period. During the period 1940 to 1968 the percentage of bills passed to bills introduced was much greater in majority parliaments. Table 5 provides a summary comparison of the seven minority government sessions and the remaining twenty-five sessions of majority government. While some majority government sessions have performance ratios below the average of 3.3 for minority governments, on average it required almost an extra day to pass a bill in a minority government session, and the performance ratio dropped to 3.3 compared to 4.1 during majority governments.

The downward trend in law-making performance and the specific lack of efficiency during minority governments may be accounted for by the increasing complexity in legislative interaction. Technical considerations and the variety of demands raised by interest groups have contributed to the increasing intricacy of bills, estimates and other matters. Minority governments compound the impact of such demands by requiring the government to entertain more withinputs from the minor parties. Since electoral studies and public opinion polls indicate that minority governments are likely to recur, reform proposals must counsel the type of institutional change which will promote high levels of performance even in the face of the increased complexity of inputs and withinputs in the legislative system.

THE CONSEQUENCES OF A REFORM POLICY

The above statistics are instructive about law-making efficiency in the House of Commons, but they do not provide any firm conclusions about how particular reforms will affect performance. To accomplish that objective the effects of policy changes on performance must be examined. An attempt to change the procedures of the House was made during 1968 and 1969. It constituted a positional policy because it was aimed at affecting the process of policy-making rather than any substantive policy in that process. The evaluation of its effect on the performance of legislative decision-making provides an introduction to the problems of evaluating reform policies.[12]

In this section we will limit the discussion to an evaluation of the success which the 1968–69 policy achieved in reaching its objectives. There are, of course, problems in deciding precisely what those objectives were. While general agreement may be obtained on the need for a new policy, there are usually different opinions about the goals and values that it embodies. For example, it might be argued that the major objective of the rule changes was to allow a more thorough legislative scrutiny of government proposals, or that it was to allow the government to meet its legislative commitments, or that it was both.

It is reasonable in this case to examine the objectives of the government since the final policy embodied only those reforms it felt were acceptable. The content of government objectives has been summarized by Donald S. Macdonald.[13] Unfortunately, his criticisms of the legislature were more explicit than his articulation of government objectives. Part of the reason may have been a desire to avoid discussing government intentions and to emphasize the role of Parliament within the context of the new rules. According to Macdonald, there had been too much "politicking" in Parliament and not enough attention to the careful examination of bills. The House had been too slow, members were bored by long, tedious sessions, and all of this was attracting public criticism. In his opinion the new rules would be designed to alleviate these problems.

Buried in these criticisms and proposals were three objectives. The first and primary objective was of intermediate range. The government wished to improve the performance ratio of the House of Commons. While it was not stated boldly by Macdonald, his explanation of the rule changes dwells heavily on the effect of protracted debates on government business. The proposals also embodied two short-range objectives intended to help accomplish the primary goal. First, the imposition of time restrictions on particular debates and the removal of repetitive and unnecessary motions was intended to give the House more time to debate public bills. Second, the abolition of Committee of Supply, the radical curtailment of Committee of the Whole and the automatic referral of most bills to standing committees on second reading, was intended to delegate a major proportion of the legislative workload to the committee system. The House was considered an inappropriate forum for some types of decision-making and it was assumed that even though the new procedures would be more complicated, any disadvantages would be outweighed by the opportunity to have many items considered simultaneously. This would also increase legislative performance.

It is important to be aware of unintended consequences, particularly in the case of the second of these short-term objectives. The justifications the government offered for the rule changes did not include a clear statement of what was expected of the committee system. The Special Committee on Procedure (1967–68) which initiated the policy seemed preoccupied with improving proceedings in the chamber rather than the committee system. Almost no steps were taken to prepare committees for the anticipated increase in workload. In assessing the impact of the reform it is therefore necessary to examine the performance of the committee system under the new procedures. The most suitable way to test the impact of a policy is to perform a controlled experiment where the stimulus is properly isolated and changes in performance may be attributed to its influence. In the case of parliamentary reform this approach is impossible. The only feasible procedure is to examine in some detail two sessions of Parliament, one before and one after the new rules, and determine if the variation in performance can be attributed to the reforms. In general terms these sessions illustrate the impact of a revitalized committee system.

The earlier discussion of Table 4 noted that an increase in legislative performance occurred immediately after the introduction of the provisional rule changes in 1965, followed by another increase in the 28th Parliament. However, neither increase was particularly dramatic and the latter came at a time when a majority government succeeded six sessions of minorities. Table 6 indicates that during the four sessions since the rule changes were adopted the performance ratio has remained, on average, lower than that recorded during the sessions between 1945 and 1968. Together these findings suggest that the intermediate objective of improving the performance ratio of the legislature met with little immediate success.

Table 6: COMPARISON OF LAW-MAKING PERFORMANCE, BY SESSION, 1945–1968 AND 1968–1972

	Average no. of sitting days	Average no. of public bills enacted	Average no. of days to pass a bill	Average no. of pages of enacted legislation	Average no. of pages passed per sitting day
1945-68	110.6	48.3	2.5	428.0	3.9
1968-72	171.3	54.3	3.3	629.0	3.7

SOURCE: *Debates of the House of Commons; Statutes of Canada.*

This conclusion does not mean, however, that the policy failed to achieve its short-range objectives. There is some indication that the goal of making more time available to the legislature for law-making was quite successful. The second session of the 27th Parliament and the second session of the 28th Parliament each lasted 155 days; but in the latter session, after the rule changes, many more hours were devoted to public bills on the floor of the House of Commons. The abolition of the Committee of Supply, the virtual abandonment of the Committee of the Whole, and the elimination of redundant motions combined to provide the House of Commons with more time to devote to legislation.

The second short-range objective seems to have succeeded as well. As anticipated, there was a dramatic increase in the activity of the committee system between the two sessions examined. One of the most obvious bases of comparison is simply the number of meetings that were held in each of these sessions. In the second session of the 27th Parliament the committees held 218 meetings (excluding sub-committees and meetings adjourned because of lack of quorum) but in the second session of the 28th Parliament 759 meetings were held. In the earlier session, while 21 committees were constituted, only 13 of them ever met. In the second session of the 28th Parliament each of the 18 committees met at least three times and one committee met over one hundred times. Similarly, in the second session of the 27th Parliament no meetings at all were scheduled during three months (April, August and September), whereas in the later session at least one committee held meetings every month. Not only were committees more active than before 1968, but this activity was distributed more evenly throughout the committee system, and committees utilized more of the time available during the year.

Table 7 indicates that only 93 pages of legislation were considered by committee in the second session of the 27th Parliament compared with a total of 461 in the second session of the 28th Parliament. Even considering that the number of active committees had increased, the average committee in the later session considered about twice as much legislation as in the earlier session. Given this heavy increase in overall workload, it is tempting to speculate that one reason the reforms did not provide a higher performance ratio for the legislature was the inability of the committee system to consider and return bills to the House promptly. However, when the performance ratio is calculated in terms of the number of hours of committee time devoted to the consideration of one page of legislation it reveals an improvement in committee performance. In the second session of the 27th Parliament only six committees considered and reported legislation and for some committees it was a lengthy operation.[14] The performance ratio of the committee system during this session was 1.9, whereas in the second session of the 28th Parliament the performance ratio of the committee system became .83 as the committees were forced to handle a massive increase in workload (see Table 7). Our analysis indicates that the government achieved the objective of transferring the consideration of legislation to committees without sacrificing efficiency in the sessions examined.

Table 7: A COMPARISON OF THE ACTIVITIES AND LAW-MAKING PERFORMANCE OF THE COMMITTEE SYSTEM IN 2ND SESSION, 27TH PARLIAMENT AND 2ND SESSION, 28TH PARLIAMENT

	2nd session 27th Parliament	2nd session 28th Parliament
No. of bills considered	18	86
Total volume in pages	93	461
Time spent examining bills (hours)	177	401
Ratio of time (hours) to volume (pages)	1.9	0.83

SOURCE: *Proceedings of the Standing Committees.*

Limiting our discussion to legislation ignores estimates and other miscellaneous items which constitute a major part of committee activity. They are undeniably part of a committee's workload but in this case a volume measure is less appropriate.

While the volume of legislation may be accurately depicted by the number of pages of legislation, the amount of time spent dealing with estimates and miscellaneous items is a better indication of workload for these topics.

As mentioned previously, the number of sitting days in the two sessions under consideration was 155. When one turns to the time devoted to the study of departmental estimates during these two sessions the effects of the 1968 procedural changes are immediately evident. As Table 8 indicates there is no means of comparing the amount of time spent in Committee of Supply for each session, since that body was no longer operative in the later session. However, the table shows that transferring the bulk of estimates examination to the committee system resulted in the investment of an extra 74 hours to the consideration of supply. The study of estimates in committee required approximately the same length of time as it did on the floor of the House in the earlier session. The additional hours in the later session were consumed by opposition motions under Standing Order 58. It might be argued

Table 8: COMPARISON OF TIME SPENT ON ESTIMATES BEFORE AND AFTER THE 1968 RULE CHANGES

	2nd session 27th Parliament	2nd session 28th Parliament
No. of sitting days	155	155
No. of hours spent in Committee of Supply*	205	0
No. of hours spent on estimates in standing committee	46	219
No. of hours spent debating supply motions (S.O. 58)	0	106
Total time spent on estimates (hours)	251	325

SOURCE: *Debates of the House of Commons; Proceedings of Standing Committees.*

*Includes six, two-day supply motions.

that debates under Standing Order 58 do not apply to the study of estimates and therefore should not be included. However, such debates were intended to compensate for the loss of opportunity to challenge governmental policies during Committee of Supply and during the debates on supply motions. By transferring the consideration of supply to committee and retaining for the opposition an opportunity to initiate resolutions under the heading of "Supply" in the House, there was an absolute increase in the amount of time Parliament devoted to this aspect of surveillance.

The unanticipated consequences of reform were almost as significant as the desired changes. The rules fostered duplication in the subject matter discussed. There was a tendency to repeat at report stage in the House debates that had already taken place in committee. The nature of committee proceedings also seems to have changed. In the second session of the 27th Parliament the number of hours of committee time devoted to the examination of legislation comprised 54 per cent of the total, but in the second session of the 28th Parliament this had dropped to 28 per cent of the total, despite a rather significant absolute increase (see Table 9). It is in handling miscellaneous items that the committees have spent most of their time—61 per cent in the later session compared with 32 per cent in the earlier one. Those items assembled under this heading include annual reports, white papers, the Auditor General's report and general investigatory references. This finding is of considerable importance since it represents a marked change in the nature of committee activities that cannot be traced directly to procedural changes. The procedural changes which specified that both bills and estimates must be referred to standing committees have had the effect of strengthening the committee system and making it a more viable structure for the handling of general investigatory references. It is in this latter quarter that the committee system seems to have enjoyed the greatest expansion in activities.

The 1969 rule changes succeeded in providing the House with extra time to debate legislation and in transferring the detailed work on bills, estimates and other matters from the

Table 9: COMPARISON OF THE AMOUNT OF TIME DEVOTED TO TYPES OF COMMITTEE BUSINESS, 2ND SESSION 27TH PARLIAMENT AND 2ND SESSION 28TH PARLIAMENT*

	2nd session 27th Parliament		2nd session 28th Parliament	
Bills	177 hrs.	(54%)	401 hrs.	(28%)
Estimates	46 hrs.	(15%)	219 hrs.	(14%)
Miscellaneous	104 hrs.	(32%)	950 hrs.	(61%)
TOTAL	327 hrs.	(101%)	1570 hrs.	(101%)

SOURCE: *Proceedings of the Standing Committees.*

*Figures have been rounded to the nearest hour and percentages to the nearest whole number.

House to the committees. In the short term it even improved the legislative performance of the House, but the performance level returned to its pre-1968 standard in subsequent sessions. The new procedures have been unable to dramatically reverse the trend toward lower performance ratios which was caused by the impact of intricate legislation and the prevalence of minority governments. The reforms produced considerable decentralization and proliferation of structures, but also allowed greater opportunities to obstruct the flow of legislation.

Given these constraints it may be difficult to affect radically the level of legislative performance through reform measures. But the greatest problem with evaluating either the performance of the House of Commons or attempts to reform its activities is the absence of standards. Until Canadian politicians decide what Parliament should achieve, scientific evaluation of legislative performance will continue to be a process of short uncertain steps.

NOTES

1. Robert Dahl, "The Evaluation of Political Systems" in I. de Sola Pool, ed., *Contemporary Political Science: Toward Empirical Theory* (Toronto: McGraw-Hill Co., 1967), pp. 166-81; David Easton, "The New Revolution in Political Science,"

American Political Science Review, Vol. 63, no. 4 (December 1969), p. 1052; Eugene Meehan, *Contemporary Political Thought: A Critical Study* (Homewood, Ill.: Dorsey Press, 1967), p. 230 and p. 232; Harry Eckstein, *The Evaluation of Political Performance* (Beverly Hills, Calif.: Sage Publications Inc., 1971); and Ted Gurr and Muriel McClelland, *Political Performance: A Twelve Nation Study* (Beverly Hills, Calif.: Sage Publications Inc., 1971).

2. Evaluation may also imply an examination of unintended as well as intended consequences, an evaluation of the objectives themselves, or an attempt to ascertain why a particular policy met with success or failure. See Edward Suchman, *Evaluative Research* (Hartford, Conn.: Russell Sage Foundation, 1967), Chapter 3.
3. John Saloma III, *Congress and the New Politics* (Boston: Little, Brown, 1970), p. 5.
4. Roger Davidson, David Kovenock, and Michael O'Leary, *Congress in Crisis: Politics and Congressional Reform* (Belmont, Calif.: Wadsworth Publishing Co. 1966), p. 2.
5. Only one author has explicitly grappled with this problem in Canada. J. A. A. Lovink suggests five criteria which may be used to evaluate reform proposals. The criteria he suggests amount to five activities the author feels Parliament engages in, or should engage in. His evaluation of the impact reform proposals may have on these activities is an impressionistic one in the sense that he relies on no indicators beyond his own judgment. Lovink succeeds in covering many aspects of legislative performance but not in such a manner that others may repeat his exercise and expect to arrive at his conclusions. See Lovink, "Parliamentary Reform and Governmental Effectiveness in Canada," *Canadian Public Administration*, Vol. 16, no. 1 (Spring 1973), pp. 35-54.
6. Suchman, *op. cit.*, p. 12.
7. Dahl, *op. cit.*, p. 174.
8. Abraham Kaplan, *The Conduct of Inquiry* (Scranton, Penn.: Chandler, 1964), p. 176.
9. Pages were used as an indicator of volume rather than bills because they constitute a more precise measure and because bills receive clause-by-clause scrutiny.
10. A moving average tends to even out the trend line, but the danger lies in the tendency of moving averages to find a trend where none may actually exist.
11. James March and Herbert Simon, *Organizations* (New York: John Wiley, 1958), p. 183.
12. The inherent values of the researcher are among the most persistent of the difficulties involved in evaluating policy. There

seems to be a widespread tendency among social scientists in liberal democracies to believe that doing something is better than doing nothing on almost any occasion. Furthermore, there is a tendency to ignore the unanticipated consequences of those changes which are approved of on moral grounds.

13. Donald S. Macdonald, "Change in the House of Commons: New Rules," *Canadian Public Administration*, Vol. 13, no. 1 (Spring 1970), pp. 30-39.
14. The Standing Committee on Labour, for example, required twenty-one meetings to consider one bill, four pages in length —and this after the bill had received approval in principle. It might be argued that among the reasons for this lengthy process was the simple desire of the committee to continue to have meetings since it was unlikely that it would receive another reference during the session.

9. Reform Design: Politicians and Policy-Making

The first seven chapters have established the relations between the legislative system and society, the inner circle and Parliament, the House of Commons and its committees, and the political actors and the roles they attempt to assume. Chapter 8 aggregated the data on members' activities by assessing legislative and committee performance. While more research would be helpful, the preceding synthesis has suggested deficiencies in the legislative system and has permitted observations which may be useful in prescribing change. All legislative reform is circumscribed by two important facts. First, no government will accept procedural changes no matter what theoretical justification is provided unless it is assured that changes favourable to the interests of the government will also be adopted. Secondly, it is reasonably simple to adjust procedures and institutions, but immensely difficult to initiate change which has a positive effect on performance levels. In our opinion only comprehensive adjustments in the linkages and the institutions can enhance the significance of the legislative system.

Since incrementalism often leads to contradictory proposals, consistent reform depends on an articulation and a commitment to long-range objectives. At this juncture in the development of Canadian parliamentary institutions there should be three objectives to reform:

1. *To improve the linkages within the legislative system.* Insufficient concern is shown for relations between the executive and legislative branches. Academics and political practitioners are too inclined toward a rigid separation of the functions of these two structures. Moreover, the new pattern of alternating majority-minority governments compounds existing weaknesses.

2. *To increase the policy-making role of the individual MP within the legislative system.* Reshaping the role of parliamentarians should not be at the expense of executive and political control. Attempts to make Parliament into the major policy-making forum or to diminish the resources of the inner circle are unlikely to be helpful, but more political input at the appropriate stages in policy-making is essential.
3. *To enhance the image of Parliament in the mass public.* Parliament will have to adapt to innovation in society, in particular to the new information technology.

These objectives will require the elimination of some old structures, the adjustment of some procedures, and the creation of some new institutions. There will be obstacles to the realization of the objectives and these impediments to change will be discussed after the reform proposals are outlined.

EXECUTIVE–LEGISLATIVE LINKAGES

There should be a restructuring of some institutions in the pre-parliamentary stages of the legislative system. In Canada the linkages have not been rationalized so that the stages for producing legislative items and the stages within the House are coherent. There are two essential areas for reform: the organization and preparation of the executive's approach to Parliament and the approach itself.

The preparation of executive action has been aided by general goals, but ministers have not been committed to using them to force departmental response in the form of legislation. In fact, there has been some tendency to regard policy as separable from the legislative program. Some organizational changes would be helpful. In addition to instructing departments to list their legislative proposals in correspondence with government goals, an inventory of departmental legislation which has fulfilled established goals should be circulated within the public service. In Britain the ministries prepare documents for their ministers on how to implement the party platform. Such a practice would be a salutary, if sometimes embarrassing, addition to policy-making in Canada.

In the preparation of the legislative program departments

are too independent of cabinet control despite the efforts of the Privy Council Office. On occasion departments even circumvent cabinet intentions on the program. Fail-safe technical procedures have not been developed, and sometimes the government has found itself with insufficient legislation to place before Parliament. Draft bills are not circulated among departments and, consequently, some policy considerations are often raised too late in the process. Lastly, no satisfactory means has yet been developed to allow feedback from parliamentary institutions into this process.

The solution of those difficulties associated with the preparation of the legislative program lies in a more thorough coordination of departmental policy memos and the drafting process, and more political input from ministers, caucus and parliamentary institutions. The most direct means of producing such a result would be to appoint one minister responsible for the entire legislative system. Since modern government requires the Prime Minister to organize all the coordinating agencies, this new role should be assumed by another minister supported by a powerful cabinet committee structure. The responsibilities of the Cabinet Committee on Legislation and House Planning should be increased. It should control the legislative program and form a bridge between Parliament and the cabinet. To discharge these responsibilities the structure of the committee should be changed to provide for a Future Legislation Committee and a Current Legislation Committee. Ideally, the new responsible minister would be the chairman of both committees and also Government House Leader. While he would have no departmental legislation to pilot through the House, he would be responsible for the composite program and its political thrust. This minister could retain the formal title of President of the Privy Council or the presently unassigned position of Minister of State could be made the vehicle for this structural change.

Upon cabinet approval of priorities the minister would request from his colleagues legislative proposals which conform to government objectives. The minister's planning staff would perform the administrative duties now carried out by some sectors of the PCO. Plans for scheduling activities in departments and in parliament would be drawn up concurrently. The overall government priorities would, of course, remain the responsibility of the Cabinet Committee on Priority and Planning, serviced by the PCO. The administrative duties of the Government House Leader, such as office allocation, would be transferred to the Government Chief Whip. The drafting office of the Department of Justice should be made responsible to the new minister's department, but it should be attached to Parliament for administrative purposes. The new drafting office should be expected to act as a service agency for central government. It should draft bills according to the priorities set by the Future Legislation Committee or, in exceptional situations, by the Government Leader in the House. Draft bills should be immediately circulated for departmental consideration and the departmental solicitors should be drawn into a comprehensive framework for the legal consideration of all bills.

The Future Legislation Committee would design the legislative program one year in advance of the session for which it was to be used.[1] The committee would receive advice from the departments, the PCO, draftsmen, the Chief Government Whip, and the new minister's staff. This information would determine (subject to cabinet confirmation) the size of the program and the actual items to be included. If the committee rejected a bill, the sponsoring minister would be required to appear before the committee to argue for a reconsideration. Such an arrangement would limit departmental autonomy and individual ministerial control. The Future Legislation Committee could also supervise the writing of the Speech from the Throne. The chairman would have to be a tenacious administrator, however, since the integrity of the committee would depend on adherence to the shape and schedule of the legislative program as originally approved by cabinet.

The Current Legislation Committee would be assigned many of the tasks now undertaken by the Cabinet Committee on Legislation and House Planning. As in the United Kingdom, the new committee should not be required to examine the draft bills clause by clause to locate drafting errors. The sponsoring department, the drafting office, and the chairman's staff should advise the committee of the major political difficulties in the legislation (especially those that might prove embarrassing in the House) and help in the scrutiny of all projected expenditures and wide delegations of power. For practical and tactical purposes the precise timetable for the introduction and processing of legislation in the House should be left to the Government House Leader and Chief Whip, who would act in accordance with the wishes of the Prime Minister.

In order to improve executive–legislative linkages the government should cultivate some new practices and attitudes in its approach to the House. Even though the new minister responsible for legislation would become the main link between the executive and the legislature, the administration of the Whip's Office could be improved and the Government Chief Whip should be elevated to the status of a junior minister to permit his attendance at cabinet meetings on legislation. The House Leader's meeting should remain the focal point of party negotiation, but a business committee composed of House leaders and the chairmen of standing committees should coordinate activities in the parliamentary part of the legislative system. The government should provide Parliament with its own legislative schedule much farther in advance than is presently the case. Parliamentary planning should be based on a monthly rather than a weekly announcement. Items should not be added to the program during a session unless they are for extreme emergencies or unless they can be handled by a Second Reading Committee as discussed below. The addition of legislative items during a session diminishes the relation between goals, priorities and bills, and ignores the need for adequate communication with Parliament.

The government should return to the practice of placing a list of legislative proposals in the Speech from the Throne. It should inaugurate a clear distinction between types of government publications by tabling green papers to illustrate government "ideas" and white papers on clear government "policy." Experiments with other types of papers will only harm public understanding of the policy process. Marc Lalonde's orange paper on social security in the 29th Parliament was an example. The practice of introducing trial "balloon" bills should also be dropped, to indicate the government's seriousness in developing a disciplined approach to the legislative program.

The executive should respond to initiatives from Parliament and its committees. Substantive reports from parliamentary committees, for example, should be considered in departments, and ministers should provide answers to the criticisms and suggestions. This could be accomplished by the tabling of government green papers in response to House proposals. The government currently informs the Public Accounts Committee what action it has taken on its recommendations. It should extend this practice by explaining the reasons why it has not been able to accept the recommendations. The links with the House should be seen as feed-back mechanisms in which the executive absorbs ideas from the House in the same way as Parliament reacts to cabinet initiatives.

INSTITUTIONS IN PARLIAMENT

Reform in Parliament should focus on those activities and institutions in which individual participation and organizational efficiency can be improved. Sympathy is widespread for the efforts of individual MPs who wish to satisfy personal aspirations and bring ideas to bear on the art of governing. Perhaps less obvious is the need for increased efficiency in the conduct of parliamentary business. Some proponents of parliamentary reform even consider it to be a contradictory goal.

There are two reasons for suggesting that efficiency, a value associated with the executive, be maximized in a reform of parliamentary proceedings. The first is a practical one. The government will be unwilling to permit the adjustment of parliamentary structures if no government priority is recognized. The idea of permitting free votes on the floor of the House or unlimited debate in committee would be opposed by any government because neither reform offers an incentive for abandoning the status quo. The second reason is that within a parliamentary system the political executive, the cabinet, must assume responsibility for managing the affairs of the legislature. Procedures that permit the government to avoid its responsibilities will have undesirable ramifications in the pre-parliamentary part of the system. They will also make it more difficult to assign responsibility for policy and hence will undermine the principle of democratic accountability. The government will not be made more responsive by making it more difficult to pass legislation. Political control of the legislative system requires that cabinet be provided with the means of achieving its legislative objectives.

The size of the House of Commons is too small for the legislative and constituency workload of members. It should be enlarged so that no member will represent more than fifty thousand constituents. Moreover, sessions of the House of Commons last too long, making it difficult for most members of Parliament to maintain permanent contact with their constituencies. Sessions should be roughly equivalent in length. They should begin in the fall and, if possible, be shortened. In the legislative process itself no speeches should last more than thirty minutes. A Second Reading Committee should be established to process legislation which House leaders agree is non-contentious.[2] These reforms would provide Parliament with more time for legislation on the floor of the House. To further expedite business, Parliament should agree to end the procedure whereby those bills which have not been passed during one session die on the order paper and must be reintroduced at the beginning of the next session. This is a process which inevitably results in the duplication of effort and permits the government to introduce trial "balloon" bills which they may have no intention of passing. Parliamentarians have the right to expect the government to remain committed to items that are on the legislative program. Failure to pass a bill should be a comment on the government's program, not on parliamentary inefficiency.

The government ought to have the means of terminating an opposition filibuster of legislation without recourse to closure. The present unfortunate wording of standing orders 75A, 75B, and 75C may not permit the government to set its own time limit. In fact, it may be possible for opposition parties under 75B to impose their time allocation on a majority government. On the strength of parliamentary convention, the government should be a party to any agreement regarding parliamentary time and appropriate changes are required to realize this objective.

The function of surveillance is served neither by the lengthy Throne Speech Debate nor by the Budget Debate, which is interrupted by the resumption of normal parliamentary business. Some of the time presently devoted to these debates could be reassigned to the discussion of matters raised in committees. Even Standing Order 43, which is occasionally a useful means of forcing debate, should have a time limit imposed on it.

Oral question period is presently a forum for unrelated assertions of fact and opinion. Order and continuity is required and for this purpose Parliament should adopt, with some amendments, the British practice. This would terminate spontaneous questions by stipulating that those which require an oral reply must be on the order paper at least forty-eight hours in advance. The preparation of both queries and replies would thus become much more methodical. Members would still be motivated by political considerations, but questions would have to be worded carefully to solicit facts unflattering to the government. Excessive outbursts would either be ruled out of order or easily circumvented by an experienced minister. Replies would be drafted by departmental officials, but members would retain the right to ask a limited number of supplementaries. Ministers would no longer be able to stall their antagonists by arguing that considerable time is required to assemble the information. Members would lose the privilege of giving immediate expression to their inspirations, but the House would be saved the interruptions of the Speaker's rulings and the inequities of a system in which most members are recognized by the speed with which they spring to their feet. The new arrangement would be enhanced if certain days were set aside for the discussion of particular ministries or particular policy areas. However, matters of urgency would not be dealt with immediately (placing more pressure on Standing Order 43), and it would be advisable, therefore, to supplement the revised question period with the present practice of permitting party leaders to initiate questions on contemporary issues. Beginning with the Leader of the Opposition each party should be permitted a single spontaneous question with supplementaries. It is anticipated that the retention of this feature of parliamentary questioning in Canada would further emphasize the clash between the Prime Minister and opposition party leadership.

The government should establish a continuous review of private members' bills and decisions should be taken regularly on which bills deserve to be passed. Precedence on the order paper should be established by a ballot among all members. Bills that are accorded priority and are discussed during private members' hour should be voted on at second reading. If they secure passage at this stage the committee system would provide a means by which MPs could solicit the opinions of the ministers and public servants responsible for the areas covered by the bill. If a bill is rejected at second reading the sponsoring member should be provided with an explanation of government policy and the reasons for the refusal. Private members' motions should be selected by a similar ballot procedure and be regarded as resolutions of the House, expressions of opinion not binding on the government. These motions should be permitted to come to a vote without the whip being applied. If they are adopted the government would not be formally required to act, but moral suasion would have been applied and backbenchers would have been granted another point of access in the legislative system.

The proposed changes are designed to rationalize and develop the main opportunities for efficiency and participation within the parliamentary part of the legislative system. The House of Commons requires, in addition, a pre-parliamentary policy-making capability. The denial of any formative policy-making role will probably hinder the performance of other ascribed functions. However, Parliament cannot satisfy a policy-making role by perfecting tactics of legislative obstruction or by altering the policies which have already undergone detailed formulation and to which the government is openly committed. Policy input, if there is to be any, must come at a much earlier stage and certainly before legislation is within Parliament. The committee system of the House of Commons has the most potential for this type of reform and a comprehensive alternative can be offered in this area.

A multi-functional committee system has been described earlier as one in which each committee is expected to assume responsibility for a variety of activities. In contrast to a system like Britain's, in which one committee is responsible for the parliamentary stages of law-making in a policy area while another is responsible for scrutiny and surveillance, a multi-functional system has numerous subject-matter committees in which members acquire an expertise in all facets of a single policy area. Ideally, each activity should be executed when it is most likely to have an impact on the government and interested publics. In Canada, however, general investigation is often undertaken and advice offered when committees are ostensibly engaged in law-making. This means that the government's legislative program is delayed while witnesses are called and the committee investigates. Yet legislation is one of the final stages of policy-making and when a majority government is committed to legislation few major changes are ever achieved by backbenchers.

Canada should retain a multi-functional standing committee system but investigation and advice should occur in the policy-creation stages. Committees often make valuable contributions to the refinement of legislation and they should retain the opportunity to offer detailed amendments. Research has shown, however, that over half the members of the 28th Parliament believed that the committee system had no impact on policy formation.[3] In response to this situation committee institutions should be developed so that members of Parliament may participate in long-term indicative planning. That is, the institutions should provide opportunities for backbench input into the government's goals and priorities. Moreover, adjustments in legislation and the criticism of spending patterns should be based on a comprehensive understanding of government policy in a particular area. The floor of the House, however, would remain the scene of eloquent debate and political manoeuvre.

To accomplish these objectives legislation should go to committee with narrow terms of reference and, in all but the most exceptional situations, with no provision for other than departmental witnesses to be summoned. Committees examining legislation should be charged, as they are in Britain, with the task of debating and amending details. The informal business committee, discussed earlier, should decide on the length of time each bill requires in standing committee. In short, the committee system should prepare itself to handle the government's legislative program in a thorough and expeditious manner. For its part, the government should formulate a projected legislative schedule including the demands it intends to make on parliamentary and committee time for the consideration of legislation.

Committees should be assisted in acquiring a much larger role in investigation. This can be accomplished partly through the existing estimates procedure, but new opportunities should be provided for members to initiate investigations into selected policy areas. Committees should automatically be granted wide terms of reference at the beginning of each session, and the government should refer to committees the annual reports of all departments in order to give substance to these general references. If the experience of British select committees is an indication, the Canadian committees will choose issues and areas on which no firm policy commitments have been made by any party. Where possible the government should also table statements of policy intent in the form of green papers. It is envisaged that when the estimates are tabled the committees will have already chosen areas of concentration and members will have become sufficiently conversant with policy that a more effective surveillance function can be performed. The estimates should be referred to the normal subject-matter committee with an Order which will allow for the investigation of government policy and the possibility of examining estimates on a comparative basis. The royal recommendations on bills should be drafted in wider terms with only total expenditure included in order to provide procedural flexibility.

A more specialized committee system requires government response to parliamentary initiatives. Procedures should be introduced to permit the discussion of committee reports on the floor of the House. Substantive committee reports should have concurrence moved and be debated during a specific committee time. In this regard consideration should be given to alloting a specified number of "committee days" per session and permitting the Speaker to choose the committee reports to be debated. Concurrence in such reports would not render them binding on the government. Nevertheless, the government should respond automatically to them by tabling a paper explaining why it agrees or disagrees with the recommendations. This would initiate another round of pre-legislative policy study within committee.

A committee system which offers expanded opportunities for personal initiative would encourage the continuity in membership necessary for specialization. Even with an enlarged House of Commons, it would be desirable to reduce the number of members on each committee, particularly the two thirty-member committees. To retain flexibility in membership change and at the same time discipline the procedure, members should be permitted to change committees only on a quarterly basis. Adjustments in the number of standing committees should be made to reflect governmental reorganization rather than to lower the level of membership turnover.

Leadership in committees should be institutionalized. On the government side the role of partisan leader should be assumed by the parliamentary secretary who may have to be accorded some of the rights and duties of a junior minister. The chairman should be made an impartial official and a panel of chairmen should be created with the government and the opposition each providing half the delegation. The Speaker should be empowered to select chairmen from among the panel to serve on particular committees. The chairmen would administer research funds and represent committees in the House but only on the direction of a majority of committee members. In a system which would place heavy emphasis on investigation and scrutiny, an impartial chairman would encourage cooperation among all members of the House. He would occupy a position of authority not effectively influenced by the government. Moreover, a panel of impartial chairmen, acting as a unit, may be able to secure important concessions from the government that are unobtainable by individual plea.

A professional research staff and a budget for committees are necessary additions to this type of committee system. Recent studies indicate that the lack of support facilities, including research assistance is the most common complaint voiced by members.[4] Presumably the fixed budget is the more radical feature of this research scheme since it would provide the committee with the funds necessary to launch an independent investigation. The research staff could be attached to the Research Branch of the Library of Parliament, but it should be assigned specifically to committee work. These reforms would have a cumulative effect on committees inasmuch as they would provide a new and separate source of information and an opportunity to conduct affairs with less fear of government interference.

THE LEGISLATIVE SYSTEM AND SOCIETY

Changes in the committee system could increase the ability of members to contribute to policy-making and provide the government with an opportunity to conduct its business in a more orderly fashion. It is also possible that the type of improvements suggested will enhance the image of Parliament among the mass public. As we have emphasized throughout, a reservoir of support for Parliament is necessary for the performance of ascribed functions. Unfortunately, the impact of internal reforms on public attitudes toward Parliament is difficult to assess. Even when efforts are consciously undertaken to improve Parliament's status the problem of evaluating the impact remains. This does not mean that reforms should not be made, only that their consequences, intended and unintended, ought to be carefully considered.

Committees should be encouraged to increase, not curtail their travelling. When committees meet in different surroundings citizens can see their representatives at work. Travel also stimulates a more thorough development of the subject-matter specialization on which the committee system should be predicated. Radio and television should be used to announce committee meetings and invite submissions. Witnesses who appear before parliamentary committees should be selected by a steering committee on which all parties are represented. Decisions of this committee should be made public by listing those who will be granted, and those who will be denied, access to committee deliberations. Parliament should investigate the protections available to witnesses in committee hearings. When sensitive personal matters are under discussion the committee should consider accepting only sworn testimony or holding in camera meetings.

It is reasonable to assume that the image of the individual member of Parliament would be enhanced if Parliament were to adopt strict legislation in the area of conflict of interest. Conflict of interest legislation should clearly establish that membership in the House of Commons is a full-time activity. Those private financial interests a member retains should be carefully supervised by a parliamentary committee and by the courts. A green paper outlining detailed legislation on conflict of interest for members of Parliament was tabled in the House of Commons in July 1973. A similar set of stringent requirements should be imposed upon cabinet ministers and public servants because they are extremely vulnerable to conflicts of interest in the legislative system. Codes of ethics cannot replace legislation in this field.

Election expenditure by parties and candidates is increasing more rapidly than the cost of living. In January 1974 Parliament approved an election expense formula with quite high ceilings and rather weak supervisory mechanisms. It is to be hoped that over time inflation will reduce the impact of the allotments and that the officers appointed to oversee the regulations will be scrupulous in their endeavours to keep down election expenses and to plug any loop-holes that may arise. If these factors are not present public cynicism toward the legislative system may be a by-product.

One means of encouraging devotion to parliamentary duties is to provide a level of remuneration high enough that members of Parliament can remain independent of private sources of income. There is little excuse for the undignified controversy that surrounds every pay increase. After the 1972 salary raise MPs receive a fixed, taxable salary of $18,000 with an additional $8,000 of non-taxable income. In the future salaries should be automatically adjusted according to an economic indicator which reliably reflects the increase in wages and prices. In keeping with the government's own policy on taxable income, no provision for non-taxable funds should be included in the new formula. It is true that the needs of MPs differ and that not everyone requires additional research or secretarial aid. Nevertheless, as the Beaupré Report emphasized, a general improvement in the standard of facilities would probably increase the effectiveness of all MPs. The early 1974 decision to provide constituency offices for members of Parliament was a step in the right direction. These offices should help to relieve the burden of requests and referrals to government agencies and will symbolize the member's continual role in the constituency. However, the members need even more executive and technical support. Each member should have a research assistant both in Parliament and in the constituency. These should be formal positions, not secretarial allotments. During election campaigns offices in public buildings should be provided for both incumbents and challengers.

In communicating with the mass public, institutions and individuals in the legislative system rely heavily on the mass media. Members of Parliament are usually anxious to present their views to an attentive radio or television audience while the government saves many of its most poignant announcements for the television cameras, much to the dismay of parliamentarians eager to provide a rebuttal. The time when an educated man could nourish his political interests by examining Hansard has passed. Now members of Parliament must compete for attention with members of the parliamentary press gallery who provide the bulk of parliamentary comment. On television there are programs which usurp the role of politicians. Even the titles of some programs such as Question Period and Ombudsman are adopted from parliamentary institutions. If Parliament is to be the centre of the political communications network, a means of communicating directly with the mass public is required.

On June 30, 1972, the Standing Committee on Procedure and Organization presented a report on the prospects of broadcasting and televising House of Commons' debates. The committee recommended an experiment in closed circuit television and this rather cautious suggestion is a minimum practical step toward the improvement of communication. Certainly the introduction of live televised debates would signal many changes in the parliamentary part of the legislative system; oral question period could not remain in its present state, many procedures would require clarification and some would require amendment. Of course, the advent of television could have unanticipated and undesirable consequences for the relationship between the legislative system and society. There is a danger that debate would lack spontaneity and that some members would endeavour to monopolize attention. Since about 80 per cent of the proceedings are in English, the French audience could resent the translation and more cabinet ministers would be obliged to confine parliamentary remarks to the French language. Some of these difficulties may be overcome by existing legislative norms, but Parliament should carefully supervise the conditions under which debates or events are televised. Parliament should televise its own proceedings with its own technicians but allow broadcasters to employ the tapes and sound tracks as they wish. A national cable television system should carry all parliamentary proceedings in the expectation that if Parliament is widely projected a large audience could be educated in the fundamentals of government and support for parliamentary institutions could be generated.[5]

Finally, Parliament requires an association of parliamentary authorities, politicians, academics and members of the public to promote interest in and informal debate on parliamentary government. Canada is one of the few democracies without a journal of opinion about its parliamentary institutions. In the United Kingdom the Hansard Society presently assumes this task in addition to providing a forum for discussion about governmental reform. A Canadian institution could undertake similar duties and possibly even share responsibility for projects such as the Parliamentary Interns program.

IMPEDIMENTS TO REFORM

There is little reason to believe that in the future political authorities in Canada will be more able than they have been in the past to reform parliamentary government or to abandon an ad hoc approach to the resolution of political issues. Many politicians are sceptical of the virtues and the possibilities of comprehensive change. Public policy may not be determined solely by environmental factors, but political, cultural and societal cleavages and social and economic realities restrain all actors in the legislative system from embarking either on long-term policy-making or major institutional reform.

The inertia in Canadian politics is compounded by the behaviour of political parties and interest groups. In a political system where interest group demands are highly valued, public policy-making may deteriorate into the negotiation of private group claims. Interest groups will seek to prompt, adjust or halt piecemeal change on a variety of issues. In combination with backbenchers and provincial governments they can restrict the political choices of the executive. Detailed knowledge of particular policies and the authority acquired from their membership permit interest group leaders to make representations to the government which are more compelling than those of members of Parliament.

Political parties similarly recognize little advantage in pursuing national policies based on competing value systems. In Canada the parties often converge in their attitudes toward sectional and ethnic cleavages and traditional left-right divisions seem inappropriate to the discussion of many political issues. These factors have a depressing effect on the style of opposition offered in the Canadian Parliament. The opposition represents an alternative set of individuals, rarely ideas. If, as Bernard Crick maintains, the modern Parliament should resemble a permanent election campaign, then the major combatants will be obliged to articulate consistent policy positions on an array of political issues. For the moment such a development appears unlikely.

Apart from these fundamental impediments to change there are obstacles to innovation within the legislative system itself. While many former MPs seek other public offices upon defeat or retirement, politics in Canada sometimes appears to be an ephemeral sport engaged in by those who have the available time and resources. The rate of attrition among Canadian members of Parliament remains high by British and American standards, and Canada lacks a large core of experienced parliamentarians. In liberal democracies schemes to improve the calibre of politicians are sometimes frowned upon, but it is rather utopian to expect a reforming zeal and a commitment to parliamentary institutions from politicians whose relationship to the legislative system is often short-lived.

The attitudes and values of both elected and unelected participants also constitute obstacles to reform. Actors in the legislative system often show a reluctance to undertake any type of institutional change. Bureaucrats have a distinctive and necessary policy-making role in the legislative system, but they remain protective of their realms of authority. Employing the canons of administrative secrecy and guarding their "territory" is a preoccupation of officials even at the highest echelons of government. In Parliament there is also a tendency for politicians to protect revered institutions. Any increase in institutional autonomy, for example, is frequently regarded as a challenge to the parliamentary form of government. Neither members nor ministers seem particularly inclined to conceive of Parliament as a feedback mechanism to the executive or to consider the functions the legislative system may perform in society. And yet reform proposals must be premised on a strengthening of these relationships.

Experience indicates that reform of the legislative system in Canada will be a spasmodic affair. When the strains of workload and antiquated procedures finally appear to lower performance levels, the government will react with reforms designed to alleviate the immediate causes. This penchant for short-term amendment can be traced, in part, to electoral necessity. Policies are almost always evaluated in terms of their electoral appeal and politicians are understandably reluctant to think beyond the next election. Minority governments, in particular, focus attention on survival and the short term. Parliamentarians are normally resistant to change but, in minority situations, governments are especially reluctant to further complicate relationships by reforms that affect the rules of the game.

The unwillingness of Canadian politicians to plan major policy change is related to their reluctance to change existing institutional arrangements. Institutions are most appropriate when they give expression to the policy-making models bureaucrats and politicians accept. Now, however, as interdependence increases in Canadian society and as the interrelationships among societal problems become visible, the need for planned change and institutions capable of providing it will become more pressing. In the legislative system improving the relationship among goals, priorities and the legislative program is crucial to long-term policy-making. But the grim prospect is that fundamental impediments in society and obstacles in the legislative system will continue to militate against a comprehensive and coherent restructuring of the role of politicians in our policy-making institutions.

NOTES

1. A similar cabinet committee in the United Kingdom aided the Labour government to accomplish its enormous legislative program between 1945 and 1951.
2. This structure would diminish the need for those omnibus bills which are used solely to link minor adjustments in the law.
3. Michael Rush, "The Committees of the Canadian House of Commons," unpublished paper, 1973.
4. J. A. A. Lovink, "Who Wants Parliamentary Reform?", *op. cit.*, p. 510.
5. Canada might consider adopting the computerized answering service now employed in the State of New York for those citizens who want extra information about parliamentary proceedings.

Index